PRAISE FOR *WHATEVER THE COST*

"The Benham boys have got it down straight! True worship to the Almighty is living it out loud every single day. They also have the right attitude about enduring persecution for the sake of the kingdom. Welcome to the frontline, boys!"

—PHIL ROBERTSON, THE DUCK COMMANDER AND ROBERTSON FAMILY PATRIARCH FROM A&E'S *DUCK DYNASTY*

"The Benham brothers are taking the words *double trouble* and turning them into a double blessing! As an evangelist, my heart pounds when God's people proclaim the salvation message, and the Benhams do just that. This battle call will have you pick up your armor and fight, no matter the cost."

—CHRISTINE CAINE, FOUNDER, THE A21 CAMPAIGN; AND BEST-SELLING AUTHOR, *UNSTOPPABLE*

"As a father of nineteen children (and counting) and a Christian businessman, I so appreciate how the Benham brothers have energized my faith and encouraged me to stand boldly for Jesus, whatever the cost! Their stories are real, their humility evident, and their courage compelling. This book will be a staple in our home. Well done, boys!"

—JIM BOB DUGGAR, FATHER, *19 KIDS & COUNTING*

"They simply don't make men like the Benham brothers anymore. And that's the point. Their story will shake you and wake you, motivating the courageous way of living your soul longs for but, until now, never found its way out."

—GABE LYONS, FOUNDER, Q IDEAS; AND AUTHOR, *THE NEXT CHRISTIANS*

"This book is a road map for cultural impact! The Benham brothers are open and honest about the failures and victories in their lives that are dedicated to serving Christ. I loved the specific how-tos that are laid out for those wanting to get out of their comfort zones. This book inspired me and challenged me not to shrink back in the face of opposition. I'd run with these boys into battle anytime and anywhere."

—AL ROBERTSON, PASTOR AND OLDEST, BEARDLESS BROTHER, A&E'S *DUCK DYNASTY*

"Reading *Whatever the Cost* inspires me to have hope for this generation if we can reproduce change agents like Jason and David. Their story provides hope that we can turn things around if we, like they, live a Christianity in obedience, whatever the cost. These two young men model godly choices from which each of us can learn and gain much wisdom. Read this book, and then give it to every kid in his twenties. Perhaps we can foster more Jasons and Davids before it's too late. Well done, guys!"

—Os Hillman, president, Marketplace Leaders; and author, *Change Agent* and *TGIF, Today God Is First*

"Full of wit and wisdom the Benhams teach and encourage us to live a fully integrated life pleasing to God, regardless of the cost. The way they uncover the identity of workplace Christians as ministers on mission is life-changing. Their unique mission concept—missioneering—provides an out-of-the-box way to bring the gospel to the world!"

—Ken Eldred, CEO, Living Stones Foundation; and author, *The Integrated Life*

"*Wow!* This is a remarkable story of a family committed to living for God, whatever the cost. David and Jason bring to mind the words of Sir William Wallace: 'Every man dies. Not every man really lives.' The Benham brothers are truly living life abundantly as they refuse to sit on the sideline or shrink back from the epic clash of worldviews that unfolds before us. They are standing resolute for the truth of the gospel. I can't wait to read the sequel as God uses them to stir the hearts of the next generation."

—Tony Perkins, president, Family Research Council

"You can promote homosexuality, pornography, profanity, bigotry toward faith, degradation of women in explicit song lyrics, and recreational drug use with impunity, but God help you if you put in a good word for God. In *Whatever the Cost* the Benhams provide us with a living testimony of two guys who weren't afraid to speak out—no matter the cost. I know you'll enjoy their stories, but you also will be moved to display similar courage in standing for what is right."

—Mike Huckabee, former Arkansas governor; host, *Huckabee*, Fox News; and best-selling author

"This book challenged me from chapter one! Insightful and thought provoking, the Benhams will challenge your integrity and self-discipline, then leave you fired up to live your faith."

—ALEX KENDRICK, WRITER, DIRECTOR, AND
ACTOR, *LOVE DARE* AND *COURAGEOUS*

"Jason and David Benham are the enemy's worst nightmare. Their steadfast faith, unwavering commitment to God, and unashamed zeal for His Word are a serious threat to the kingdom of darkness in our culture. This book is meant to do exactly what I've personally discovered a face-to-face encounter with its authors does: galvanize believers to fervent faith and action. It will be a divine antagonist to your soul—disintegrating spiritual apathy and sparking an internal fire that will burn long after the last page has been turned. You will love this book, and it will mark you forever."

—PRISCILLA SHIRER, BIBLE TEACHER AND AUTHOR

"David and Jason Benham are the latest targets of the out-of-control cultural police. By taking a stand for family values, the Benham brothers may have lost a television program, but they gained the respect of millions who believe in free speech and in standing up for your principles. While the media worked overtime to make the Benhams look like members of the Westboro Baptist Church, I found them to be solid Christian men who love all people and accept their differences. I am proud to call them friends and encourage you to read their story because there are many important lessons you can pull from their experience."

—GLENN BECK, BEST-SELLING AUTHOR, *DREAMERS*
AND DECEIVERS; AND FOUNDER, THEBLAZE

"Amazing things happen when you keep your priorities straight. God. Family. Integrity. Financial wisdom. Generosity. These are the keys to winning, but too many people get it wrong and drive their whole lives off a cliff. In *Whatever the Cost*, David and Jason show you how to achieve incredible success by making God and family the cornerstones of your life."

—DAVE RAMSEY, *NEW YORK TIMES* BEST-SELLING AUTHOR
AND NATIONALLY SYNDICATED RADIO SHOW HOST

"David and Jason Benham are not only identical twin brothers; they have experienced life's ups and downs together. *Whatever the Cost* is a good read for the entire family. Why? It demonstrates the responsibility parents have to teach their children the power of God's Word, and it challenges teenagers and young adults to build their lives on the strong foundation of biblical truth.

"These guys write about the thrill of seeing their dream become reality—being drafted by Major League Baseball—and describe the disappointment of their careers being cut short, having no idea what to do next. But through it all, they learned that faithfulness isn't proven in the exhilarating times of life but in the ordinary.

"This fast-paced story is chock-full of fun, brotherly rivalry, and the competing personalities of two guys working together to build a business that was on its way to becoming a popular reality TV show—until the plug was pulled. They learned that there is often a high price to pay when speaking God's truth in love. You will be moved with compassion and challenged with resolve to stand on the firm foundation of God's Word—whatever the cost!"

—FRANKLIN GRAHAM, PRESIDENT AND CEO, BILLY GRAHAM
EVANGELISTIC ASSOCIATION AND SAMARITAN'S PURSE

WHATEVER
THE COST

WHATEVER
THE COST

FACING YOUR FEARS, DYING TO YOUR
DREAMS, AND LIVING POWERFULLY

DAVID AND JASON BENHAM
WITH SCOTT LAMB

W PUBLISHING GROUP

AN IMPRINT OF THOMAS NELSON

Published in Nashville, Tennessee, by W Publishing Group, an imprint of Thomas Nelson.

Published in association with the literary agency of WTA Services, LLC, Franklin, TN.

Thomas Nelson titles may be purchased in bulk for educational, business, fund-raising, or sales promotional use. For information, please e-mail SpecialMarkets@ThomasNelson.com.

Unless otherwise noted, Scripture quotations in this book are taken from the New American Standard Bible®, © 1960, 1962, 1963, 1968, 1971, 1972, 1973, 1975, 1977, 1995 by The Lockman Foundation. Used by permission.

Scripture quotations marked NKJV are taken from the New King James Version®. © 1982 by Thomas Nelson, Inc. Used by permission. All rights reserved.

Scripture quotations marked NLV are taken from the Holy Bible, New Life Version. © 1969, 2003 by Christian Literature International, P.O. Box 777, Canby, OR 97013. All rights reserved.

Scripture quotations marked NLT are taken from the Holy Bible, New Living Translation. © 1996, 2004, 2007 by Tyndale House Foundation. Used by permission of Tyndale House Publishers Inc., Carol Stream, IL 60188. All rights reserved.

Scripture quotations marked NIV are taken from the Holy Bible, New International Version®, NIV®. © 1973, 1978, 1984, 2011 by Biblica, Inc.™ Used by permission of Zondervan. All rights reserved worldwide.

All italics in Scripture quotations were added by the authors for emphasis.

Library of Congress Control Number: 2014918834

ISBN 978-0-7180-3299-9

Printed in the United States of America

15 16 17 18 19 RRD 9 8 7 6 5 4 3

To my brother:

Oh, wait a second—that's really weird. Scratch that.

To our kids:

Bailey, Ty, Ella, Ava, and Chase (David's kids); Trae, Allie, Jake, and Lundi (Jason's kids). You're all the spice of life. What an honor to be called your dad—or uncle, depending on which one of you is reading this.

To our wives:

Lori (David's wife) and Tori (Jason's wife). You both played hard to get, but your little tactics obviously didn't work well. We're better men because of you. We both out-kicked our coverage.

To Mom and Dad:

For all the years of trying to figure out which one of us was your favorite. Mom, enjoy reading this curled up in your blanket by the space heater. Dad, settle in on your little green kitchen stool with a box of Fudgsicles and read away.

Cowardice asks the question, is it safe?
Expediency asks the question, is it politic?
Vanity asks the question, is it popular?
But conscience asks the question, is it right?
And there comes a time when one must take a position
that is neither safe, nor politic, nor popular, but he must
take it because conscience tells him it is right.

—DR. MARTIN LUTHER KING JR.,
FEBRUARY 6, 1968, WASHINGTON, DC

CONTENTS

FOREWORD

KINGDOM MEN ARE HARD TO FIND. A KINGDOM MAN IS A MALE WHO consistently functions under the comprehensive rule of God. While men will regularly count the cost for success in the areas of athletics, business, and entertainment, their passion does not often transfer over, as it should, to the spiritual realm. This is why the Benham brothers are so refreshing. They have decided both privately and publicly to take their stand as Christians. Not willing to hang out in the closet of spiritual complacency, they have positioned themselves as beacons of light in the midst of cultural compromise and spiritual mediocrity.

In a world of saccharine celebrities—people who serve as inferior substitutes for the real thing—the Benham brothers stand as a unique model and clear representative of God's kingdom agenda, which is the visible demonstration of the comprehensive rule of God over every area of life.

The Benham brothers have uniquely wedded technical excellence and spiritual maturity in such a way that clearly demonstrates that biblical manhood is not for chumps. Rather it is the high calling God has for men who are His followers. The Benhams are not just businessmen who are Christians. They are representatives of God, diagnosed as businessmen.

To sit and speak with them personally is to witness the fire of men who have decided that cultural Christianity and religious compromise are not for them. Having counted the cost of full commitment to Christ and His kingdom, David and Jason have cast their lot with their Lord even though it has meant financial loss, public ridicule, and rejection, as well as loss in the level of fame and popularity that this world has to offer.

In *Whatever the Cost* David and Jason chronicle their story in a vibrant, exciting, and challenging way. It is a story that will challenge every reader—men and women alike—to make a total commitment to Christ. It will encourage and convict you to get off the fence and go all the way with your faith, no matter the price tag. You will also discover that the reward for total commitment, and the inevitable trials that come with it, will be well worth the inconvenience.

The Benham brothers have decided that the applause of heaven is more important than the recognition of men. They have rejected the false notion that the sacred and the secular are two independent realms to be kept separate from each other. Rather they have verbally and visibly demonstrated that God is the ruler over all of life and is not to be divorced nor marginalized by those who dare claim Him as Lord.

No matter where you are on your spiritual journey, this book is for you. Better yet, the God who inspired the writers of the book is for you. These two former baseball players want you to know that it's time for you to leave the stands, pick up your bat, go to the plate, and swing for the bleachers. There is a world out there desperate for Christ-followers, like the Benham brothers, who will pay the price, *whatever the cost.*

—Dr. Tony Evans
Senior Pastor, Oak Cliff Bible Fellowship
President, The Urban Alternative

ONE

WHAT'S ALL THE FUSS ABOUT?

Be on the alert, stand firm in the faith, act like men, be strong.
—1 Corinthians 16:13

 When your faith is under fire, it is important to remember that God uses fire to make your faith flourish. #ItsGettingHotInHere

"WE WANT YOU GUYS TO KNOW THAT WE THINK YOU'RE GOING TO BE stars on our network."

Those were the last words we heard from HGTV before getting fired the next day. Looking back, that phone conversation was the height of our reality TV career. Life for us as big-time reality TV stars was about to begin.

We had several weeks of production under our belts, and HGTV would begin airing our *Flip It Forward* show in the fall (2014). Although we didn't have long beards, a crazy uncle, or a hunting business, we were going to give those Duck boys a run for their money! At least we were gonna try.

We'll go ahead and state the obvious in case you couldn't tell from the cover of this book—we're identical twins. There's not much different about us other than the fact that each of us thinks he's better looking than the other. We love competing, talking smack, and having a lot of fun. Life's too short to be so serious all the time. So when we started filming our reality show, nothing really changed for us. We just had a bunch of cameras around now.

A few days before the network fired us, our show producer had the brilliant idea for us to carry an old toilet down the stairs and into the front yard of one of our flip houses. No problem—but which one of us was going to hold the tank, and which one was going to hold the bowl? Rock-paper-scissors worked every time when we were kids, so we did it again. I (David) won—and I chose the tank (there was no way I was carrying the bowl!). And being the loving brother that I am, I chose to walk backward down the stairs for the sake of my bowl-carrying brother.

For those of you wanting to be on reality TV, here's a tip to remember: if your show's producer can't stop smiling from ear to ear before filming a scene, you may want to ask why. Halfway down the stairs we faced the gruesome reality that our producer had left the toilet full! Once the water started spilling out of the sides, it was all she wrote for us. We barely made it down the stairs before we dropped to our knees and started dry heaving. "Hold the moment, boys! Embrace this moment. We're gonna kill 'em with this footage!" yelled our producer. We weren't interested in killer footage at that moment—we were interested in killing our producer! For nearly five weeks we did some of the craziest stuff we've ever done in a house—stuff we hadn't seen on TV before—all to embrace the exhilarating moments of house flipping. Whatever the cost, right?

During the first week of filming, one of the executives from HGTV came in town to check on the show. He was eager to take us out for a steak dinner the night he arrived, so when we wrapped filming for the day we headed uptown to get our steak on. Just before we dove into our filets, he leaned back in his chair and said, "Okay, guys, I've got to tell you: you're about to be known by millions of people. Nobody knows you right now, but very soon millions of people are going to discover you and start checking you out. We're going to reveal your show at the New York City upfronts."

Okay—that's cool, we get it. Can you pass the salt?

He continued. "We've been following your Twitter posts, and we noticed that you guys tweet a lot of stuff about your faith, and you even speak about controversial issues. We don't mind you talking about your faith, but speaking about the controversial stuff may give people the impression that you're 'haters,' and I don't want people thinking something about you that you're not."

The conversation started getting real. We tuned in a bit more closely.

"David tweeted something about your dad baptizing 'Jane Roe' of the *Roe v. Wade* Supreme Court decision." (In 1995 our dad had the privilege of leading Norma McCorvey to faith in Jesus Christ. If that name sounds familiar, it's because McCorvey is also known as "Jane Roe" from the infamous *Roe v. Wade* Supreme Court decision, which legalized abortion in the United States.)

He finished by saying, "That may be a little much right now."

At this point we stopped eating. Our appetites faded as fast as our heart rates elevated. We thought, *Oh boy, here we go again. It's coming.*

HAVE YOU EVER WONDERED WHY ALL THE FUSS ON THE EARTH? Think about it—so much turmoil, fighting, and bickering all the time. From the Middle East conflict to the bully in kindergarten to the halls of our legislature, there's always a clash—a fight taking place . . . every day.

Well, the Bible has a lot to say about this. In particular the book of Revelation sheds an incredible amount of light on all this fighting. We will talk about this more in chapter 19, but at first glance Revelation is tough to understand. Yet the overall message of the book is actually pretty simple. There are just two basic facts to remember:

1. There are two kingdoms—the kingdom of light and the kingdom of darkness—and they are in conflict. They are enemies with no option for peace. This is a fight to the death.
2. By the end of the book, one kingdom has destroyed the other—utterly and completely.

That's the message of the book of Revelation. And if you haven't guessed it by now, the kingdom of God (light) destroys the kingdom of Satan (darkness).

Nestled into the middle of the book is the scene of the original battle that started in heaven and now rages here on the earth. Satan threw the first punch and tried to take authority away from God—he wanted it all for himself. However, God defeated Satan and tossed him and his followers, angels like himself (now called demons), out of heaven. In Revelation 12:11, we read this powerful verse:

> And they overcame him because of the blood of the Lamb and because of the word of their testimony, and they did not love their life even when faced with death.

This verse serves as an explanation for how the people of God will overcome the devil.

- "because of the blood of the Lamb"—*salvation*
- "because of the word of their testimony"—*salvation lived out*
- "they did not love their life even when faced with death"— *whatever the cost*

This verse provides the three-step formula for defeating Satan when he attacks us on the earth:

First—*salvation*. All of us are sinners, and therefore we must pay the penalty for sin, which is death. But Jesus, who never sinned, took our punishment for us and stripped Satan's authority at the cross. Through salvation we become children of God—we are transferred from Satan's kingdom of darkness into God's kingdom of light. That's step one.

Second—*salvation lived out*. When we become children of God, we experience internal transformation that produces external transformation. In other words, our actions begin to reflect the kingdom of light in our lives. Living out our salvation in this way is called our testimony. It's like a witness who testifies in court because he or she has firsthand experience. Our testimony declares to the world that Jesus is both a merciful Savior and also the universal King because we've witnessed it in our own lives. That's step two.

Third—*whatever the cost*. When we live out our salvation, there will be a price to pay because the kingdom of light that now resides in our hearts stands opposed to the kingdom of darkness. We don't fit in like we used to because our lives are revealing God's authority. So Satan attacks. And when he does, we have the choice to raise the white flag or fight. The only way we'll fight is with the same attitude the angels had in heaven: *even in the face of death, I will stand*. This whatever-the-cost attitude is step three.

Our journey hasn't resulted in martyrdom, like many before us, but it is in the same spirit of Revelation 12:11 that we have approached the writing of this book. God's amazing grace and tender mercy saved us when we were young. And for the last thirty-nine years, He's built our testimony for Him—with lots of ups and downs. During those rough times when Satan attacked us, God was right there all along, forging a whatever-the-cost attitude in our hearts.

We certainly hope the title of this book doesn't make you think we're picture-perfect examples of how to live powerfully for Christ whatever the cost. You'll see in many chapters how we *didn't* get it right and how God was faithful to strengthen us to live powerfully for Him the next time around. You'll see where we failed and where we stood strong. You'll walk with us as we ambitiously jumped out ahead of God and where we faithfully let Him lead. You'll experience the roller-coaster ride of what life was like being super aggressive, hardheaded twins who needed quite a bit of restraining for most of our lives. This book is the "word of our testimony" so far.

We tried to write in the way we normally talk, so it's a bit unconventional. You'll see our personal comments and jabs at each other throughout—standard stuff for twin brothers who take their message seriously but don't take themselves too seriously. If you're anything like us, you'll skim through the pages looking for the good stuff, so we've made it easy for you by highlighting some of our life principles. These are also compiled in Appendix B for quick reference. By the time you finish reading the book, we hope to compel you to trust Jesus with your life whatever the cost, to live powerfully for Him, and to provide you with biblical principles you can apply to your life the minute you put the book down.

Hopefully, as you read our story, you'll be able to see how we lived out these principles in unique situations. Like many others we had to learn the hard way, but we're so glad we did. You'll read about competitive twins who had a dream of playing professional baseball, who did exactly that in their early twenties before having to give up the dream of making it to the big leagues. You'll see how we used biblical principles to build a successful real estate business from scratch and how you can do the same in your own work life. You'll experience the thrill of us signing a deal with HGTV for a show on flipping houses and the whirlwind of confusion brought on by the abrupt cancellation of that show because of our beliefs. You'll see the immense power wielded by certain organizations whose ultimate goal appears to be destroying others with opposing views, especially those based on the Bible. And you'll understand why we couldn't be more thankful for all that has occurred and more steadfast in our desire to live for Christ and to love others with all the conviction we have.

But to fully appreciate our story, our actions, and the principles we live by, it's important to know the background of everything that made us who we are today. So let's head back to Orlando, Florida, in 1975. Although we never rocked tennis headbands with lamb-chop sideburns and butterfly collars, we were just about to enter the scene.

TWO

CRITTERS

The Early Years (1975–1980)

I have made a fool of myself, but you drove me to it.
—2 Corinthians 12:11 NIV

 Sometimes you win, and sometimes you lose . . . but sometimes you just get rained out. When God gives you crazy kids you just gotta take what you got. #WeLoveYouMom

YOU'VE SEEN THE DISNEY MOVIE *BRAVE*, RIGHT? IN THE MOVIE there were three little boys—crazy critters—who magically turned into bear cubs. They ripped into everything and terrorized the entire palace. That was the two of us as toddlers. There's really no other way to describe it.

We're certain our parents loved us during this time in our lives, but we're not so certain they liked us much. We've got plenty of stories. It's probably a good thing we don't remember a lot of them, so we'll rely on Mom and Dad to describe just how terrible and wonderful we were.

Rocking his 1970s bell-bottomed jeans and bushy brown hair, Dad took Mom to the doctor three days before we were born, which was when they found out they were having twins.

"Her belly was huge," Dad said. "Massive. We figured we were having a giant baby."

"I couldn't fit behind the steering wheel of the car," Mom added. "So they did an X-ray and then called me at home to say there were two babies on the picture. I remember sitting down and thinking, 'Oh my word! What will this even mean?'" (Jason: Uh, Mom, it means you're about to experience the greatest blessing of your life!)

Three days later, there we were. The most adorable munchkins the world has ever seen. Or maybe not. Here's the word-for-word transcription of how Dad described us: "You were the ugliest two little guys ever seen on the face of the earth. You were all squished up together and when they got you out, we thought, 'Oh my—what's wrong with them?'"

Mom said those early months were nonstop bottles and laundry. And she couldn't even tell us apart.

She put wristbands on us labeled "Baby A" and "Baby B." Eventually she just started dressing us in different colors. David was always in blue and Jason was anything else that wasn't blue. Still today she gets us mixed up from time to time if she sees Jason wearing blue. Even we get confused when we go to Mom's for dinner and browse through old photo albums. We were so identical that our grandma made us personalized shirts. One said: "I'm David. He's Jason." The other said: "I'm Jason. He's David." That was about the only way people could tell us apart. (Jason: Today it's pretty easy to tell us apart. If you look at us on the cover of this book and your heart skips a beat, that's me. When looking at David nothing happens, so it's pretty simple.)

Then there was our older sister, Tracy. Can anyone say, Darla from *Finding Nemo*? (Sorry for all the animated movie references—can you tell we have nine kids between the two of us?) Our big sis had no reservations in showing us how she felt. One day when we were six weeks old, she waited until Mom got in the shower, took us from our crib—where we were playing quietly, of course—and stuffed us under her bed. It was an evil plan to eliminate her competition.

Mom couldn't stop the madness. As toddlers we were everywhere, into everything, and all over everyone. So she hatched a plan: put the always-moving monsters in the playpen and give them Scotch Tape. What?

Mom says we were fascinated with the stuff. We would tape ourselves and each other—and the never-ending machine of disaster stopped for a bit. Everything got quiet. It was a miracle.

To this day we still enjoy playing with tape. Just ask any of our employees and they will tell you it's a rare occasion not to catch us with tape on our fingers or stuck on our top lips. Crazy, we know—but don't blame us. It's Mom's fault.

During this time Dad owned a bar and was going to Bible college. It's not every day you get to read a sentence like that! But Grandma was there, too, helping to take care of us. Mom worked at a nursing home from 3 p.m. to 11 p.m. while Dad and Grandma watched us. Dad says he would come home from Bible school and see us playing in our sandbox, beating each other with sticks and throwing sand at each other. We're still not quite sure what Grandma was doing at the time.

Then there was the day we were playing outside, right under Dad's nose. He was exhausted, so we can't blame him for nodding off just before we found a large, concrete drainage cover. How we were able to pick it up is beyond us, but suffice it to say that we had just enough strength to lift it off the ground and drop it on Jason's big toe, cutting off the tip of it. (David: He's got an alien toe. If he's ever wearing sandals, check out his left big toe. It's a great way to tell us apart.)

In the summer of 1976, Mom and Dad packed up Tracy and the twin terrors, and we headed to Kentucky so Dad could go to Asbury Theological Seminary. For the next three years Birch Drive had no idea what hit it. Nor did the neighbors!

We'll share just one interesting story from that time. One day while Dad studied Greek, we got into the neighbor's garage. Dad was left watching the boys (mistake number one). And our neighbor had left his garage door open (mistake number two). On the floor were several bags of ready-mix concrete (mistake number three). A nearby water hose was connected and ready to be used (mistake number four). By the time Mom got home, we were washing each other's hair with concrete shampoo. As for the neighbor's garage, let's just say it provided a perfect opportunity for Dad to exercise some of the Bible lessons he had learned at seminary, making things right with those whom you've offended.

We were always getting into trouble. Mom remembers they couldn't take us anywhere because we destroyed everything. No one invited our family over for dinner. They just couldn't take the chance. We got disciplined every day. And if one of us did something, both of us got in trouble for it.

After seminary Dad packed up our 1976 black Oldsmobile Cutlass Supreme—the one with cracked white leather seats, no A/C, and broken electric windows—and took us to Dallas, Texas, to start a new church. For the next twenty-two years the walls of 621 Dawn Drive watched our story unfold.

Our new church's first Sunday service was in our house. Six people attended, which isn't bad considering we had just moved there and started the church from scratch. The only problem was that five attendees were from our family. We had one neighbor show up.

The two of us helped where we could. We stood at the door to hand out bulletins, and since there wasn't a lot of foot traffic, we needed more to do. So Dad decided to let us help him get ready for communion—like taking the bread from the bag to the plate and pouring the juice. Here's a quick lesson to those starting a home church: Don't let your four-year-old twin boys help prepare communion. Just don't do it. While Dad was arranging the living room for worship, we were in the kitchen, administering the sacraments to each other, saying, "Take. Eat . . . Take. Drink . . ." By the time Dad offered the sacraments, most of the bread had tiny bite marks on it and half the juice was gone.

Dad taught us quickly to deeply respect and honor taking communion—or, as we called it, the Lord's Supper—but he had to use some pretty strong discipline to get the point across.

As the church grew, Mom began to realize differences in us. Jason had a deep sense of private property rights, so he'd take all his toys and hide them under a sheet on his top bunk. I (David), on the other hand, had a deep sense of public property. If I wanted to play with something, whether mine or Jason's or the neighbor's, I just took it and played with it.

I (Jason) remember David never leaving me alone. If I had something, he wanted it, and if he couldn't get it, he would terrorize me. I was a poor innocent child trying to make my way in the world. He was the crazy, calculating kid. I vividly remember a time I was climbing a tree, and David, armed with a handful of darts, told me he was going to hit the limb I was sitting on. Before I could say no, I had a dart sticking in the left side of my face. Seriously, that was a bad day.

Okay, I (David) admit that was stupid, but Jason cried too easily. Mom and Dad realized pretty quickly that my personality was more dominant than his. I would get into trouble all the time and always did the talking. Jason was quieter and got his feelings hurt fairly easy.

On one occasion Dad went to Germany for a month at Christmas to do some Christian ministry with the USO there. When he came back home, Jason wouldn't have anything to do with him at all. But me? I couldn't care less.

As we grew older, Mom and Dad began to see that our individual strengths and weaknesses complemented each other very well. Fortunately for us, our parents directed our strengths and developed our weaknesses along the right path.

It's been said that one Clydesdale horse can pull up to three tons, yet two working together can pull more than ten times as much. In the early years we were nothing but double trouble. The amount of mischief we got into was more than double that of a typical kid, but help for our poor parents was just around the corner. We were about to get a full-time babysitter—our local elementary school!

THREE

YOUNG WARRIOR SPIRITS

Elementary School (1980–1986)

Foolishness is bound up in the heart of a child;
The rod of discipline will remove it far from him.
—PROVERBS 22:15

 I'd rather restrain a mustang than kick a mule—Truett Cathy, Chick-fil-A. If you gotta be kicked then you need to be kicked . . . in the rear! #Don'tNeedKicking

IF YOU'RE A PARENT, WE HOPE THIS CHAPTER ENCOURAGES YOU. Maybe at this very moment you are trying to saddle the wildest mustang (or mustangs) this side of the Mississip'. Well, we want you to know that it's going to be okay. Trust us, if you point your child(ren) toward God, you'll harness all that energy for good and not evil. If God can redeem a couple critters like us, He can do it for anyone.

We grew up in Dallas during the heyday of the hit TV show bearing the city's name, but Dad's salary didn't match that of the show's wealthy J. R. Ewing.

Starting a small church with a salary of $15,000 a year, our dad set out to change the landscape of our city. It wasn't enough for him to just *do* church—he wanted our family to *be* the church in our city, although at our young age we were making that a very difficult prospect.

Our first day of kindergarten was unforgettable. We had never been separated for any length of time, yet on this day Jason went to Mrs. Crump's class while David went to Mrs. Garner's class. For the first time in our lives, each of us had to stand on his own two feet, without a twin brother. (David: Jason was fighting back the lump in his throat. He always had to have big brother by his side.) (Jason: Um, I wasn't the one who sucked his thumb until I was eleven.)

For the first two hours we didn't like school, until our teachers said the word *recess*. That's when it all changed. Instead of this day marking the beginning of the dark days of grammar school, it began what we like to call the greatest recess dynasty in Weaver Elementary School history.

The second our feet hit the asphalt, we were back together again, this time with a mission: find and crush all competitors. We had always battled each other in the backyard or at church, but now we had an entire playground full of children ripe for the pickin'. It's crazy because neither of us said a word to each other—we just instinctively knew the battle for the school playground was on.

Today some parents would medicate kids like us. Thankfully our parents chose to guide our competitive edge and point it in the right direction. Dad taught us to embrace the spirit of competition but to do it for the glory of God and the good of others. He showed us how to leverage our competitive natures to build each other up and not tear each other down. And he explained to us that when good kids were leaders, other kids would flourish—many of whom could not stand up for themselves. Dad taught us that when his boys showed up, the bullies would be too afraid to pick on other kids.

Proverbs 29:2 says, "When those who are right with God rule, the people are glad, / but when a sinful man rules, the people have sorrow" (NLV). Dad taught us that our desire for dominion was God-given, yet it was to be used for the glory of God (not ourselves) and the good of others. Correctly harnessing this newfound spirit of competition at recess built a solid foundation for us to seek the glory of God and the good of others throughout our entire lives.

DAD SAYS THAT EVEN AT AN EARLY AGE WE DISPLAYED STRONG athletic abilities. It didn't hurt anything that he was always making us run around the block for physical fitness and to burn off extra energy. In elementary school I (David) was faster than Jason, and we were both faster than all the other kids our age. (Jason: The problem was that David never got faster. He peaked at the age of eleven.)

We know we sound a bit like Uncle Rico right now talking about our athletic exploits, but indulge us for a moment—we're going somewhere with this.

As young boys we realized God had given us a healthy dose of athletic ability—specifically, He gave us really good throwing arms. But the problem was the way in which we found this out. We started throwing rocks at cars as they passed by our house. Unfortunately for the innocent drivers, we had a crafty system of how to do it and not get caught. We'd wait until the car got four or five houses down the street and then launch a stone rocket high up in the sky. By the time it landed, the car was seven or eight houses away. The driver would never guess the missile that crashed into their car came from the adorable, little angels standing fifty or sixty yards down the street.

On one particular day a burgundy 1982 Oldsmobile Cutlass went rolling past our house. The poor guy never knew what lurked in the shadows. As the rock left David's hand, we didn't realize just how much destruction a backyard rock could do to such a beautiful car. The brake lights lit up, the reverse lights came on, and the chase began. Why we chose to run into our *own* backyard still baffles us to this day, but suffice it to say that after the driver visited Dad at the house, it was the last day we ever threw rocks at cars.

Oh, we're not done. Another memorable display of unchecked dominion, in the form of mischief, came when we were seven.

We had a friend who lived two doors down from us. During the summer we played with him all day, every day. It was the middle of July, during one of those unbearable, 100-degree Texas summer days, when we stumbled across builder's chalk line for the first time. It was lying in our yard because Dad was having our roof replaced. So we did what any normal seven-year-old twin boys would do—we tied this kid to the tree with it. We liked the guy, but we felt like he needed to be reminded of who was in charge of our block. One spool was red and the other one was blue. He looked so patriotic pressed against the tree with red and blue chalk string wrapped around him from head to toe.

"Boys! Time for lunch!" our mom shouted from the kitchen window, having no clue what we were doing. Mom calling for lunch was like a Texas farmer ringing his cattle bell, so we dropped everything and came running. There's nothing like bologna and cheese sandwiches on white Wonder Bread with a tall glass of grape Kool-Aid to wash it down on a hot summer day. And we're sure we finished it off with a MoonPie or a Star Crunch too. Gotta love the 80s.

Unfortunately for our friend, as we were in the bliss of bologna and cheese, we forgot all about him—until the knock at the door. We can still hear that knock. It was like the sound of Chuck Norris dropkicking the door. Dad opened it, and there stood this kid's mother, red-faced with rage and looking like something that jumped off the set of *Alien*. Her son stood behind her—shoulders hunched forward, dripping with sweat, soaked with tears, and red and blue stripes all over his body. He didn't have the strength to cry anymore, or even look up for that matter.

To this day we couldn't tell you what she yelled at our dad, maybe because we've repressed the emotional scars from her verbal assault. But we never tied her son to a tree again. We did, however, get a glimpse of how far in the wrong direction we could go with unguided strength.

Your greatest weakness is often an overextension of your greatest strength. To whatever degree you can be strong in one direction, you can be equally weak in the other. The key is to be pointed in the right direction with the right amount of restraint keeping your weaknesses in check.

And don't forget, we were pastor's kids. Every month our dad led the church in communion. Although he wouldn't let us help him prepare communion anymore—because of our mischief discussed earlier—we still went to the altar with our family to partake of the elements. By this time our church was meeting at a local YMCA, and Dad would use the balance beam with a sheet over it as the altar. He liked for families to come to the altar to take communion together. With the family at the altar, he would serve them the bread and quote Jesus from the Bible, saying, "Take. Eat. 'Do this in remembrance of Me'" (Luke 22:19). The problem was that when it was our family's turn to go the altar, there always seemed to be something about it that was uncontrollably funny to the two of us. We have no idea why, but when we went down front with our mom and sister, we would laugh so hard we couldn't stop. Our dad, in the meantime, would be serving each family the sacrament. By the time he came around to us, he would quietly growl something like, "I'm going to rip you guys in two when we get home . . . Take. Eat. 'Do this in remembrance of Me.'"

But it wasn't just appropriate discipline we received. Our parents also gave us words of instruction as well. A truckload of the Bible started going into our ears and hearts even before we could read. And particular moral instructions were taught—things we should and shouldn't do. For example, because so many people in our extended family had been problem drinkers and even alcoholics, Mom sat us down and made us promise we'd never drink alcohol. To this day, by God's grace and Mom's threats, we never have. She captured our hearts with the courage of conviction to stand against something that had caused so much pain along both family lines. Like our mom, parents should not be afraid to love their kids enough to push some personal conviction into their lives.

 It isn't necessary for kids to learn from the school of hard knocks. Wisdom from parents can save children a lot of heartache. A wise person learns from his mistakes, but one who is even wiser learns from someone else's.

Mom and Dad also seized every opportunity to show us positive examples to follow—people who did things the right way. If they saw someone who was worthy of emulating, they were sure to introduce us if they could.

Our dad found such a person, so he woke us up really early, packed us in the car, and took us to North Park Mall in Dallas to see him. We walked inside and joined a crowd of people lining the picture windows of one of the mall restaurants—Denny's. We were pretty jazzed about eating at Denny's until Dad told us we were just there to watch. We lined up along the window, but we didn't see anything special. Nobody stood out. No one looked any different than anyone else.

"Watch the busboy," he said to us. "Do you see him? The older man in his fifties with the white apron and hat." Finally we saw him. Next to him was a cart that he pushed down the aisle until he came to a dirty, vacant table. He slowed the cart down and analyzed the scene. He looked at his watch. He looked back at the table. Then . . . *boom!* For the next twenty seconds he painted one of the most incredible pictures of work ethic we've ever seen. It was amazing! Like something out of a cartoon, dishes went flying into one bucket, utensils into another, trash in the bag, washrags used to clean every inch of the table and chairs, and salt/pepper/sugar stationed perfectly on an immaculately cleaned table. Everything was put in proper place for the next patrons. He looked back at his watch with a sense of satisfaction and quietly strolled to the next table. Now we understood why so many people stood outside the windows—they were there to see the busboy. When he finished the table, those watching him erupted in applause. Dad looked over at us and said, "Every job is sacred. Every job is worthy of your best effort, no matter what the job is. You make it the best you can and turn it into something people are cheering about because your effort inspires them."

Who cheers for busboys at restaurants? Our dad did, and he taught us to do the same. The busboy memory continues to encourage us that every job God places in our hands must be done for the glory of the Lord. "Whatever you do, do your work heartily, as for the Lord rather than for men, knowing that from the Lord you will receive the reward of the inheritance. It is the Lord Christ whom you serve" (Colossians 3:23–24).

As Christians, our work is our worship. The Hebrew word for worship—*avodah*—is also the same word used for work.[1] Our work becomes worship when we do it with all of our might for the glory of the Lord.

Speaking of work, it was during this time in our lives that we caught the concept of working out. Notice we said *caught*. Some things are better caught than taught, and taking dominion over our bodies was definitely one of them. Our dad didn't just talk to us about working out—we watched him do it. One of the principles our dad taught us early on was that we should exercise authority over our physical bodies, including the appetite for laziness and indulgence. He said this discipline would trickle into other areas of our lives as well. This was a tough lesson to learn, but we're glad we did.

The physical disciplines we learned as young boys provided an excellent bridge to developing spiritual disciplines as young men. We learned that discipline was doing what we didn't want to do in order to accomplish what we wanted to accomplish. So at an early age, before we learned to be disciplined spiritually, we learned to be disciplined physically.

But instilling physical discipline wasn't the only example our dad gave us. Interestingly, he rarely ran empty-handed—he would have 3x5 index cards in his hand with Bible verses written on them. He used them to memorize Scripture while he was running. We learned from this example, and to this day we mix spiritual training with physical exercise. We call it our God WOD (Workout of the Day) and do it once a week with a group of guys. We do a Bible study for an hour; then we hit a workout for forty-five minutes.

Dad did more than memorize the Bible while he was running. He also said, "Jesus loves you" to every person he passed, and he picked up trash along the way. It was totally normal for Dad to show up back at the house with two handfuls of garbage. This is when his "coach shorts" played a pivotal role because he could stuff his 3x5 cards in the pockets when his hands were full.

This was how our dad modeled *being* the church for us as he served and blessed the community in which he lived. Interestingly, not long ago we received a text from an elementary school friend saying he had recently become a Christian. He said that more than thirty years later he had not forgotten the days he watched our dad run through his neighborhood and say to him, "Hey, buddy! Jesus loves you." Well, that seed finally took root, and he prayed to receive Christ. God used our dad's simple faithfulness while running through the neighborhood as a catalyst to save this man's soul. Now that's worthy of catching.

And so, during our elementary school days Dad pretty much told everyone he saw that Jesus loved them. And at the age of six we each realized that Jesus loved us too. We'll never forget bowing our heads to pray with our dad to accept Christ. It was a hot summer day, and we had just finished running around the gym. So there we were, two sweaty twin boys, bowing our heads and praying to receive Jesus. Our new lives in Christ had just begun; we had a *lot* of growing to do.

FOUR

CREATE THE CRAVE

Junior High (1986–1989)

> *Train up a child in the way he should go,*
> *Even when he is old he will not depart from it.*
> —Proverbs 22:6

 Leadership is the ability to create an appetite in those you lead. The question is, what kind of appetites are you creating? #CreateTheCrave

DAD AND MOM NEEDED A TON OF EMOTIONAL AND SPIRITUAL encouragement when we hit puberty. We already thought we were invincible—and didn't mind letting the world know it—so when larger doses of testosterone entered the mix, our parents had some serious praying to do.

One of the verses that encouraged them during this season was Proverbs 22:6: "Train up a child in the way he should go, / Even when he is old he will not depart from it." There were plenty of times they felt like nothing was working. (David: Especially when it came to Jason and Dad. Jason knew exactly what buttons to push to tick Dad off, and he loved doing it.) This verse gave our parents hope.

Dad studied Greek and Hebrew when he was in seminary, and he taught us the importance of these original languages of the Bible. Knowing the Hebrew meaning of "train up" in Proverbs 22:6 reveals the incredible wisdom of this verse. It means "to touch the palate" or "to cultivate a taste."[1]

Hebrew mothers didn't have Gerber baby food for their infants as we do today. Instead, they would simply chew up certain foods, like celery or carrots, then place a small morsel of it on the tip of their fingers, and touch the palates of their infants. This not only made it easier for the baby to gum and swallow the food, but it also activated the baby's salivary glands and created an appetite for it. Ingenious!

That's a fantastic picture of what we are to do as parents in shaping our children's morals and bending their hearts toward loving God and finding joy in Him. We shouldn't just *teach* them, but we should *train* them as well. We should touch their spiritual palates. And the best way to do this is to model it for them to see. As we parents chew on God's Word and touch our kids' palates with our lives, we will naturally create in them an appetite for God's ways. We can actually create the crave.

 We cannot give what we do not possess. It's impossible to pass on to our children something we don't truly possess ourselves. This is what it takes to create an appetite in our children for the things of God. The things that are caught are far more powerful than the things that are taught.

As young teenagers we saw our dad every morning sitting on his green stool and reading his Bible or kneeling at the couch praying. Every time we woke up, he was already there, modeling for us how men of God prepared themselves for the day. He didn't do this for show, but the sight of him there created an appetite in us to do the same thing. Both of our parents touched our palates with dozens of things during those years that created in us an appetite to be strong men.

ALTHOUGH A HUNGER FOR GOD HAD ALREADY BEGUN TO FORM inside of us at this time, we realized quickly that most things worth having don't come easy. Paul encouraged young Timothy, "Discipline yourself for the purpose of godliness" (1 Timothy 4:7). Based on this verse, our parents taught us the value of discipline early on. Dad encouraged us to set goals and then to wrap discipline around them. By his example he had already cultivated an appetite in us for two things: reading the Bible and working out. But we had a third goal as well that we didn't learn from him—to make money. So Dad helped us formulate our first three goals in life: (1) work out early and consistently, (2) read through the New Testament, and (3) start mowing lawns.

When we were in junior high, working out at 6 a.m. three mornings a week was tough. We would start the day with push-ups, sit-ups, and running. Our goal for working out was simple: to prepare ourselves physically for our careers in college and then the pros. By the time we were fifteen, we started taking turns pushing our 1967 Volkswagen Bug up and down our street. The intense burn we felt in our legs and lungs didn't stop us from continuing to push that car because the dream of making it to the big leagues was worth the pain. And the discipline to get there was slowly forming into the standard of our lives.

 You will accomplish a lot more in the pain cave than the comfort zone. The only way to maintain a disciplined lifestyle is to get comfortable with discomfort. It's like the difference between an adrenaline rush and an endorphin release. Adrenaline is the fight-or-flight feeling that happens quickly and wears off fast. An endorphin release, on the other hand, happens slowly and lasts for a long time—yet it only occurs through pain. Runners call this the "runner's high." Life is best lived off the endorphins of peace through pain and not off the adrenaline from one rush to the next.

DURING THIS TIME WE BEGAN TO EXCEL IN SPORTS, ESPECIALLY IN baseball, and Dad touched our palates with another great life lesson. Since we had strong arms and both of us pitched, we were able to shut hitters down pretty quick and roll through seasons winning most of our games. We quickly gained a reputation as the team to beat, no matter what team we were on. (Jason: I was actually carrying David in tow every year.)

When it came time to advance to the next level, all the coaches from the next division up in little league courted Dad to put us on their teams. We really wanted to play for the Phillies or the Blue Jays—perennial winners. But Dad chose the Pirates, the worst team in the league. They were like the Bad News Bears.

Dad wanted to give us firsthand experience at how to deal with losing. He knew that without learning how to lose properly we'd never know how to win properly.

 There are two ways to win: on the scoreboard and off the scoreboard. We all want to win *on* the scoreboard, but true winners win *off* the scoreboard too—which means to win over yourself. This is the most important victory. If you win on the scoreboard and lose over yourself, you've lost that day. But if you lose on the scoreboard and win over yourself, you've won that day. It's important to try to win both ways, but winning over yourself is by far the more important victory.

Joining the Pirates taught us how to lose properly—by winning over ourselves despite what the scoreboard said. It took a full season before this difficult lesson took root. In our first season we lost half our games—more losses than our previous six years combined. But the following year we set a new record for the league with thirty-three wins. Once we learned how to lose right, we were ready to win right!

But baseball wasn't our only sport, and as junior high athletes we enjoyed playing football and basketball even more. *Sports Illustrated* featured us in "Faces in the Crowd" in their May 1990 edition as two-sport athletes in football and basketball. Interestingly, it was the first time Ken Griffey Jr. graced the cover. They titled that issue "The Natural," referring to the classic baseball movie starring Robert Redford, which played a role in shaping our own baseball dreams. Even though *SI* highlighted our nonbaseball sports, we thought being in the same issue as "The Natural" could be a sign from heaven: we were going to be big leaguers!

AT A TIME WHEN WE COULD'VE EASILY GOTTEN WRAPPED UP IN OUR success as young athletes, God began to grip our hearts to draw closer to Him. We had seen our parents' sold-out commitment to Christ, and we wanted the same. Our parents reminded us that physical goals mean nothing if they don't move you toward a spiritual goal of godliness.

God has ways of deepening our commitment to Him, and oftentimes He brings people into our lives to get the message across. That's what He did for us as teenagers at a youth camp in Bastrop, Texas. Five churches and a hundred kids came together for fun and to hear messages from a "Jesus freak" camp pastor named Ken Freeman. This was in 1988, so Freeman wore old-school weight-room pants and neon T-shirts. We thought he was the coolest guy ever, and as he preached, our hearts were stirred.

I (David) put my head down and stared at the floor, and I can remember seeing tears dropping off my face and hitting the concrete. I knew I was a Christian, but I wanted to become a powerful man of God too. I wanted to give God every area of my life—I didn't want to just "be saved." I even wanted to give God my talent for playing baseball because it was the best thing I had to offer. That day I made Jesus Lord of everything, and I gave my dream of playing baseball to Him.

As the next chapter will show, God continued refining our lives in high school. But it's impossible to exaggerate the importance this early-teen spiritual experience had on us. We both heard and responded to Jesus' call to make Him Lord of our lives and to surrender everything completely to Him. This is when we first learned to die to our dreams—to focus on the things of heaven and to hold the things of earth loosely. Although we disciplined ourselves to pursue our dreams, we strived to keep them from defining us and becoming idols.

True surrender means Jesus is Savior *and* Lord. It's one thing to confess Jesus as Savior but another thing to confess Him as Lord. If He is Lord, then He is ruler of all—including our time, talents, and treasure. Jesus doesn't just want to save us and stack us up at a spiritual bus stop, waiting for Him to pick us up. He wants us to occupy until He returns. He wants us to live powerfully for Him with whatever He's given us to do, in the unique way He's equipped us to do it.

We returned home from camp with the understanding that our relationship with God was just that—a relationship. So reading His Word wasn't just some ritual we had to do as Christians, but it was the very lifeblood of a close relationship. Dad gave us a Bible reading schedule—the same one he had been using—and he challenged us by saying that if we devoted five minutes of our day to the Lord, then we had twenty-three hours and fifty-five minutes left to do whatever we wanted. Those five minutes turned to thirty minutes and then to an hour pretty quickly. And the more we read the Bible, the more principles we began applying personally.

We began to realize that the principles in the Bible held incredible truth for our daily lives. As twelve-year-olds we began mowing lawns and incorporating the principle found in Proverbs 13:11: "whoever gathers money little by little makes it grow" (NIV). By the time we were fifteen, we had saved enough money, little by little, that we were able to buy our first small business—a lawn care company with ten clients, two lawn mowers, one Weed eater, and a trailer. We were aspiring entrepreneurs and didn't even know it. Although we didn't even have driver's licenses yet, we had an income-producing business, which accomplished our third goal. We saw with our own eyes that God's principles really worked. This whet our appetites to incorporate His principles into every other area of our lives.

AS WE GREW BOTH PHYSICALLY AND SPIRITUALLY DURING THIS TIME, our family began to grow as well. During these years we welcomed our little sister, Abigail, to the world. Just two years later we welcomed our little brother, Jonathan, to our family as well. There were now seven Benhams living in our small three-bedroom home on Dawn Drive.

Our parents continued to touch our palates with truth. Dad taught us to be warriors, to never run from a fight, and to defend what was good. And to seal this lesson in our hearts he did what any good dad would do—he bought us boxing gloves. And with bright-red Sugar Ray Leonard gloves on each hand, we learned never to turn our backs on our opponent.

Maybe you haven't boxed before, but it's the most unnatural thing to keep your face set on your opponent when his fists are flying toward you. Our natural instinct was to turn away and cover up, but after sticking with it we finally started facing each other—even with fists coming our direction.

James 4:7 says, "Resist the devil, and he will flee from you." You cannot properly resist Satan unless you're willing through the power of Christ to face him first. This starts in your own life personally and then moves to your home, community, and nation. Though his fists will be flying at your face, you must never turn your back on Satan. When you face him with resistance, you have the power of God to defeat him.

Boxing became a part of our upbringing. Each Christmas we got a new pair of gloves and a reinvigorated desire to face each other. I (Jason) have a little boxing story you just have to hear. I have never been knocked out by David—not even once. David, on the other hand, cannot say the same. One day we had an epic battle in the backyard, like Rocky versus Apollo. At some point in the fight David got mad and lost control. He failed to remember Proverbs 25:28: "Like a city whose walls are broken through / is a person who lacks self-control" (NIV). He was so angry that he dropped his guard and reared back to deliver a right-handed haymaker on me, yet I kept my eyes directly on him and simply threw a right jab to his chin. Down he went, like a sack of potatoes. I've got to admit—it felt amazing. And it feels even better retelling the story. As David lay there unable to get up, I realized the importance of controlling my temper.

Of course, it was hilarious to watch, but it showed just how weak and vulnerable we can be when we lose ourselves in a moment of emotion. Dad always told us to keep ourselves under control in the middle of a fight, especially in a spiritual fight, and to never turn our backs on our opponent.

AS WE CONTINUED TO GROW AND DEVELOP FROM BOYS TO MEN, THE most important lesson our dad taught us was how to turn our theology into our biography: he showed us how to take what we believed and live it out every day. As mentioned earlier, he taught us to *be* the church and not just *go* to church. This meant that whatever God was doing in our hearts needed to show up in our actions. The church, according to Dad, was not a building but a body. And as the body of Christ, we needed to get out and be involved in our city, right where people live. For him, that meant coaching his kids in the public sports leagues, running for school board (he lost), appealing to the local convenience store to stop selling pornography (they stopped), and leading the pro-life work in our city.

These endeavors were not very popular among our dad's pastoral peers, but that didn't matter to him. And to be honest, these actions weren't popular with his kids either. We remember standing on the busiest street in our city holding signs that said, "Why thank heaven for 7-Eleven?" because they started selling pornographic magazines for the first time in our city. At the time we were more concerned about not being seen by our buddies than we were about speaking out against pornography.

We can remember one pastor telling our dad that his role was only behind the pulpit, to which our dad simply replied that his role was to impact the city and nation for Christ. Dad didn't believe the church was merely a social construct. He taught us that the church was the living body of Christ and that it was always on the move. And the moment it ceased moving forward to influence culture as salt and light (Matthew 5:13–16) was the moment it ceased to be the biblical church.

As a result of this theology, during our early-teenage years in the late 1980s, our dad started to get our church involved in pro-life work. Back then pro-life activity looked entirely different than it does today. The church's initial response to battle abortion was thousands of pastors across America blockading abortion clinic doors in attempts to save the unborn. These activities didn't last long as federal injunctions popped up everywhere. And while the methodology of protecting the unborn has changed, the importance of doing so has never been greater.

We remember all too well what it was like back in those days watching our dad get tossed around by police officers. It made a big impact on our lives. We witnessed firsthand what it was like to stand for Jesus, whatever the cost. We didn't realize it then, but watching our dad get beat up for defending the unborn created an insatiable appetite in us to become powerful men of God. We realized then and we realize now that the particular approach of protesting in which our dad was involved is not for everyone nor should it be. But we never want to lose sight of the reason for it. We all have avenues for responding to injustice in the world. The question is whether we are willing to take a stand . . . whatever the cost.

Once, we watched officers on horses dismount and begin throwing people around, and our dad was one of those people. The officers tied him and the others up and shoved them to the ground. Instead of leading him to the paddy wagon with gentleness, they stuck their police batons into the pressure points on his back. Dad winced in pain as the officers buried their thumbs in the pressure points under his jaw too. But he refused to make a sound. We thought for sure they were going to break his arms if they bent them backward any more. Several pro-lifers vomited from the pain.

All the while pro-choice crowds on the other side of the street were screaming furiously at Dad and the others. But Dad never cracked under the pressure. Whether you agree with what pro-lifers were doing at the time or not, the witness of people not loving their lives so much as to shrink back from being beaten was inspiring.

To put his theology-to-biography paradigm to the test on his boys, our dad threw us smack-dab into the middle of the ring. There was one pro-choice man who absolutely despised Dad—he would yell right in his face and scream unspeakable things. We eventually grew accustomed to this. But on one occasion while this man was yelling, Dad stood there smiling, not responding in the least. Eventually the other man calmed down and began talking in a more civil tone. It turned out the guy was a big fan of baseball and had season tickets to the Texas Rangers. So Dad had a brilliant idea: "My boys love baseball. They'd love to go to a game with you," he said with a twinkle in his eye.

You probably think our dad was crazy. Trust us; that's what we were thinking too. But the guy said, "I'd be happy to take them to a game." A few days later he came and picked us up, took us to the game, and treated us like gold. We had a blast.

Dad says he knew we were going to be safe because deep down the guy was longing for what our family had. He saw something in us that he didn't have—and he just needed to be loved. So even as kids we got to see how truth and love worked in perfect harmony.

Our junior high years were pivotal for us as we made Jesus the Lord of our lives. We learned how to build discipline around our goals, win the right way, face Satan and not turn our backs, and love the person while opposing the idea. These were lessons that were not just *taught* but *caught*. So as we entered high school, we had fully functioning appetites to live for the Lord—thanks, in large part, to our parents touching our palates with their own lives.

FIVE

INTERNAL RESTRAINT = EXTERNAL LEADERSHIP

High School Days (1990–1994)

Where there is no guidance the people fall,
But in abundance of counselors there is victory.
—Proverbs 11:14

External freedom is a result of internal restraint. The only way a kite flies is to be restrained by the string. Cut the string, down goes the kite. #HoldTheLine

BEFORE WE ENTERED HIGH SCHOOL, WE FELL IN LOVE WITH THE classic baseball movie *The Natural*. We still remember the hot summer day in Texas when our dad took us to the dollar movie theater. Little did we know how inspirational this movie would be in fueling our fire to play professional baseball. Robert Redford played Roy Hobbs, a farm boy who carved a bat out of a tree that had been struck by lightning in his yard—the very tree his dad had died under earlier that day. He named the bat "Wonder Boy" and set off all alone in pursuit of his dream to get to the big leagues. En route to his dream, however, he was sidetracked by a pretty girl and experienced something that ended his career. His dream was over. But then, eighteen years later, he came back around for one more chance at his dream. He made a big league club, and at the end of the movie (spoiler alert!), he hit the game-winning home run into the stadium lights. As the lights exploded, Hobbs ran around the bases, sparks coming down all around him, while the stadium darkened. Despite all the setbacks he had experienced, Roy had finally fulfilled his dream—in a big way. The music alone in that movie was enough to make a grown man cry. (Jason: As a matter of fact, I think I remember hearing David scream-cry at the back of the theater.)

As a pair of Texas little leaguers heading into high school, we watched that movie thinking our dream was being played out on the big screen. Yet we didn't realize at the time that, like young Roy Hobbs, our unbridled spirits could easily sidetrack us. We still had a lot to learn about life and all the temptations and folly of being aggressive, goal-driven boys.

It's rare that a couple of high school athletes would call a coach or teacher their best friend, but that's what Coach Littleton was to us. He was our football coach, and he had a huge impact on our lives. Now, before we get ahead of ourselves, we don't want you to think he was all "hey buddy, ol' pal" with us at first. Actually, he was relentless. (Jason: I still have a twitch to prove it.)

Tracy attended Garland Christian Academy three years before we arrived. Coach Littleton had been her junior high Bible teacher, and she would give him the scouting report on just how good her little brothers were at sports. He figured this was just an older sister's exaggerated belief in her brothers. After a few years of her consistent bragging, he finally met us, out on the football field.

He needed a quarterback for the football team, so he had all the players line up to throw. When it came time for us, we told him to scoot farther back than the thirty-five yards he had stood for everyone else.

He laughed at our arrogance but walked back another ten yards. As the ball sailed over his head, he just kept staring at us.

He recognized our athletic abilities and knew that relentless coaching was going to make us better—much better. Although the politically correct "softer" approach to coaching was becoming popular at the time, Coach Littleton knew he had to stay on us like white on rice. We learned quickly that face masks weren't for protecting players—they were for coaches to drag players around the field.

Going into the ninth grade, we thought we cut the string with Coach (since he was a junior high teacher), until we realized that he was taking over the high school Bible department and was moving up with us! We thought we were free, but God wanted him holding our line all four years of high school too. Don't you just love that?

Coach Littleton became the mentor who helped shape who we are today. He was on us every day, all day. He would tell us that he was going to smash us, run us until we puked, and that we were "dork-brains" (really). We had nowhere to hide, but we knew he loved us because he was willing to step into our lives and get dirty with all our stuff. From that point on, Dad and Coach Littleton teamed up to keep us on the straight and narrow. Dad was on us at home and Coach Littleton was on us at school—both men holding our kite strings tightly.

At school Coach Littleton taught Bible, logic, debate, and English. He taught us to love literature and the Bible. He taught us how to debate and defend our faith. He saw something in us beyond athletic ability and determined to train us to be leaders. Between his influence and our dad's, we moved from reading just the New Testament every year to reading through the whole Bible.

Coach Littleton showed us tough love, but as we matured he was able to shape us in other ways—less painful ways. He pulled us aside during the summer before our senior year and laid out a leadership challenge to us. He said, "You've always risen as leaders, but you've never consistently acted like leaders. Now it's time for you both to step up your game." He gave us a list of some practical things he wanted us to do for our entire senior year: (1) show up to class early, (2) sit on the front row, and (3) wear a shirt and tie all year.

At first we thought he had gone crazy. But then we realized our leadership influence in other areas could flow from this new starting point. So we agreed to the challenge, and by the end of our senior year, several other guys in the school were wearing ties.

Oh, and by the way, remember us telling you we were in *Sports Illustrated*? It was Coach Littleton who had written to them and said, "I've got some special kids you need to see." He was our teacher, mentor, and coach, and he was constantly working behind the scenes for us. But he didn't want us to know that, primarily because he didn't want us to get big heads.

ALTHOUGH WE LOVED PLAYING ALL SPORTS, IT WAS OUR DREAM TO make it to Major League Baseball that motivated our relentless approach to physical discipline. Both our dad and Coach Littleton hammered home the importance of daily discipline in shaping our athletic talents.

 Dreams don't accomplish themselves. It requires discipline to make your dream a reality. When a baseball player hits a 95 mph fastball, he's able to do this through endless hours of disciplined practice. Everyone dreams, but not everyone accomplishes. The difference is in personal discipline.

Dallas is a mecca for high school baseball. The city's large 5A public schools produce some of the top baseball players in the nation. Playing for these schools is a sure means of getting scouted by collegiate and Major League Baseball teams. Our private high school, Garland Christian Academy, however, didn't even have a baseball field at the time and was possibly the smallest school in the city. We practiced in the corner of the football field and played an all-away schedule. At this time travel ball wasn't what it is today. Back then high school ball was the place where amateur talent got recognized. But how do you get recognized if your school is tiny and you don't even have a field? Would scouts ever hear about us?

We decided that if we were going to make it to the next level, we needed to go to public school for our junior and senior years. (Jason: I know what you're thinking: *But what about Coach Littleton?* We were so blinded by our ambition that we were willing to leave him at GCA.) Mom had different plans. Although Dad was starting to be swayed by our ambition, Mom told him, "You've told those boys that God will get them where they need to go, but now for the sake of baseball, you'll pull them out of the school where they've matured like fruit on the vine?" Mom put her foot down, Dad course-corrected, and we were told to bloom where we were planted.

As we focus on depth, God will handle breadth. Our one role is to go deep with God and be faithful right where He has planted us. We don't need to worry about how wide or high our branches are going to grow—we just need to focus on how deep our roots go. He'll handle the breadth of our branches as we focus on depth in Him.

So we stayed at GCA, and that's when something remarkable happened. GCA is a small private school—we had fifty-two seniors in our graduating class. How would we ever get college and professional scouts to take a look? We did the only thing we knew to do—we prayed for a miracle!

Enter Dr. Alan Streett. Dr. Streett decided to put his homeschooling son, Aaron, on our baseball team at GCA in our junior year. Because we were such a small school, we needed all the players we could get, so we welcomed homeschoolers. Aaron played with us that year while his dad sat up in the stands watching us play and doing paperwork. Dr. Streett was a theology professor, pastor, and writer by trade.

God's ways are not man's ways (Isaiah 55:8), and God uses the "foolish things of the world to shame the wise" (1 Corinthians 1:27). We may not have had scouts watching us our junior year in high school, but we had a seminary professor!

Dr. Streett asked Dad, "Have your sons considered playing ball in college or professionally?" Dad told him that certainly was our dream, but we had no idea how it was going to happen. Without telling us, Dr. Streett decided to pen a letter to *Collegiate Baseball*, an important magazine used by scouts to locate prospects.

 God always pays for what He orders. As He orders your steps, He will work behind the scenes for you to make the way. And He does it in ways and with people you would never imagine. All you have to do is trust Him and be at rest.

Collegiate Baseball published an annual Mizuno All-American Team, in which they featured the top high school baseball players from every state. Dr. Streett wanted to submit our stats for the list, but he knew that wouldn't be enough all by itself. So he contacted an MLB scout with the Baltimore Orioles. Unbeknownst to us, Dr. Streett had some baseball success in his background, so he was well respected by some in the scouting community. A few days later he received a letter of recommendation for the Benham brothers, based on Dr. Streett's personal opinion of our abilities. Armed with a letter of recommendation from the O's and a page full of statistics on us, Dr. Streett submitted our names to *Collegiate Baseball*. (David: Let that soak in for a minute. We had no idea that we were practicing and playing in front of the man who was God's direct answer to our prayers.)

You can probably guess where this is headed. Before our senior season, we were touted as "Mizuno Top Prospects" for 1993–1994 in the pages of *Collegiate Baseball* magazine, and by then several other publications took notice and included us on their top-prospects lists as well. The first game our senior year we hopped off the bus and six major league scouts were there to watch us play. It was a miracle, and God used a seminary professor to make it happen!

God not only directed our steps toward fulfilling our dreams, but He was also protecting us from getting sidetracked along the way. As God used Alan Streett to drive us in front of the scouts, He used Coach Littleton to keep us from crashing to the ground. Unlike Roy Hobbs, we were not alone in our journey.

We began to recognize God working through people on our behalf to accomplish His purpose, and it compelled us to want to draw closer to Him. And the more we did, the more we realized that our talents were to be used for His glory and not our own. At the beginning of our senior season, baseball took on a whole new meaning.

 Your talent can be either a tool or a toy. Glorifying God with your talent makes it a useful tool. Glorifying yourself with your talent makes it a useless toy. Tools help others. Toys help only you. God wants our talents to be His tools, not our toys.

SIX

LIBERTY U

College Days (1994–1998)

Where the Spirit of the Lord is, there is liberty.
—2 Corinthians 3:17

 Liberty isn't the right to do what you *want*—it's the responsibility to do what you *ought*. And it's a great school too! #GoLU

HIGH SCHOOL WAS GOING GREAT, BUT IT WOULDN'T LAST FOREVER. The days of Saran-Wrapping cars, toilet-papering houses, and hosting garage sales in unsuspecting teachers' yards would soon be at an end. College was the next logical step, but the question was, how were we going to pay for it? By this time Dad had given up his pastoral salary in order to lead a national pro-life ministry that didn't pay much better. Since our parents barely had two nickels to rub together (it was tough feeding growing twin boys with hollow legs), our dad started praying for full-ride baseball scholarships. Of course, unless you are a left-handed pitcher who can throw the ball ninety miles an hour, you don't typically get a full scholarship in baseball.

Through the recognition we received in several baseball publications, made possible by a faithful man God brought to us, several MLB teams scouted us our senior year. We enjoyed watching Dad fill out the scouts' questionnaire cards during our games, with his trademark big black Bible tucked up under his left arm. (David: We always wondered what the scouts thought of that.) They were glad to hear we hadn't signed with any college yet and were curious to know whether we would sign with their teams if drafted. We received letters of interest from the Orioles, Red Sox, Cardinals, Mets, and Rangers. Dad probably would've considered letting us sign with a team, but Mom wouldn't allow it.

The only problem was that colleges had not bothered to scout us yet. A lot of the standout players in Dallas had already committed to big schools like Florida, Texas, and Tennessee, but it was nothing but tumbleweed blowing in the wind for us. We played before the advance of social media and YouTube, so we weren't going to get noticed unless college scouts attended our games. But they never did because our school was so small. We needed another miracle.

Everything started working itself out once Dad got arrested again. We know, it sounds odd, but that's how we grew up. It was typical for us to come home and ask Mom where Dad was. She often responded, "He's in jail again. I think he was praying at a government building or something this time." The funniest part of it all is that when Dad was in jail, every night was movie night! We actually enjoyed it—to a point.

So one night in 1993, as Dad was sitting in jail, *The Old-Time Gospel Hour*, hosted by Dr. Jerry Falwell, came on the TV. Dad's ears perked up when Dr. Falwell talked about how proud he was of the Liberty University baseball team. Dr. Falwell, the founder of the school, said they had made it to the NCAA College Regionals and were playing against Georgia Tech in the first round. We didn't even know that Liberty had a baseball team, let alone that they were playing at the NCAA Division I level.

Dad's one phone call from jail was to us. "Hey guys, I'm here in jail, watching Jerry Falwell on TV, and he says Liberty University has a Division I baseball team that made it to the Regionals. That's only a few wins away from the NCAA World Series!" We were blown away—a Christian university? How had we not heard about this before? Right then, we knew that's where we wanted to go. This was the place our talents could be sharpened into tools for God's glory.

Dad remembers getting off the phone with us and kneeling down to pray that God would open the door for his boys to play baseball at Liberty. Imagine that picture—a dad, sitting in jail without a dime in his pocket, crying out in desperation for his boys and having no hope but in Jesus. That's a pretty safe place to be.

Once again our chief ally and letter writer Alan Streett caught wind of our conversation with Dad and picked up his pen on our behalf. Dr. Streett typically wrote columns, papers, and books about theology, but this time God used him to write a letter to Liberty's head baseball coach, Johnny Hunton. His letter said something like, "We've never met. I'm a theology professor, not a baseball scout. But I know two high school seniors here in Dallas you need to sign. The pro scouts want them, but you've got to come and see them yourself. Come quickly before another school notices them. You won't regret it."

Why would Johnny Hunton care about what a minister in Texas had to say about small-potato Christian high school baseball talent? Streett enclosed a few articles on us and the reference letter from the Orioles' scout. He exhorted Coach Hunton, "You need to sign these guys to full-ride scholarships. It's the only way you'll get them."

Coach Hunton probably received hundreds of letters like this through the years, but apparently there was something about this one that felt different to him. So he jumped on a plane and flew out to Dallas. He spent two days with us, checking out our home life, church life, and baseball life. We'll never forget watching him fall asleep at the lunch table after church. (Jason: Watching him fall asleep while David was talking his ear off was hysterical.)

What we didn't realize at the time, which he told us later, was that he didn't fly all the way to Dallas to simply verify our ability on the diamond. He wanted to see if our character was greater than our athletic talent. (Hats off to Coach Hunton for being an example to all coaches: putting character above talent.)

The goal of sports is first to develop character and second to develop talent. The more coaches and parents understand this, the more competition will build others up and not tear others down. The same holds true for education—the goal is first to develop character and then to deliver content.

After Coach Hunton's nap on Sunday, the following Monday he watched us play against the number-one team in the state. Fortunately for us and by God's design, the stands were packed with MLB scouts. As God would have it, a New York Mets regional cross-checker was there, watching us play, so Coach Hunton was able to see our momentum with the scouts firsthand. You couldn't draw it up any better. It was as though God was serving His miracle to us on a silver platter. As soon as we got home, Coach Hunton pulled out two letters of intent to play baseball at Liberty University . . . on full-ride scholarships!

God answers prayer! We didn't pay a dime for college. A normal dad putting his two sons through private college at the same time would have had to earn a six-figure income at the time. But in the bottom of the ninth, God answered the prayer of a desperate dad by hitting a walk-off home run for our family.

The goal of prayer is not to simply get an answer from God—it's to get to know the God of the answer. Drawing near to God in prayer develops a relational connection that forges our union with Him in stone. And when He answers in a big way—it's just icing on the cake!

WE ARRIVED AT LIBERTY IN THE FALL OF 1994 AND GRADUATED IN the spring of 1998. We still remember our very first day at Liberty. Determined to continue the same discipline we learned in high school, we woke up at 5 a.m. for a workout before heading off to class. Since nothing was open that early, we had to climb the fence to get to the track. Well, Coach Sam Rutigliano, LU's football coach and former Cleveland Browns head coach, caught us midclimb and barked orders to get off the fence. Embarrassed, we climbed down. Two months later he called us into his office. Fearing what he might say to us about the fence incident, we discovered that he was actually looking for us to play on his football team. But that's a story for another time.

While at Liberty we forged lifelong friendships we still have to this day. It's funny to see some of our closest friends in influential positions in our culture today. When we see them, we think back to the days we launched water balloons at innocent moviegoers, hid in car trunks to get through the guard shack past curfew, and jumped into mosh pits spurred on by the "Liberty Noise." I (David) also met my wife, Lori, there. All told, our time at Liberty was invaluable, even with a strict dress code in place.

One of the most important lessons we learned while at Liberty was from Dr. Falwell himself. "If it's Christian, it ought to be better," he always said. This lesson stuck with us and played a pivotal role in developing our business/ministry paradigm several years after we graduated.

 Christians in the marketplace—or anywhere for that matter—should be characterized by excellence. When a hair stylist shares the gospel while cutting hair, which part is ministry: sharing the gospel or cutting the hair? We say *both*. Excellence in business provides a solid platform for incredible ministry.

Okay, let's get back to baseball for a minute. At this point we should stop and answer a question we get asked a lot. It goes something like this: "We know you guys are identical in appearance, but on the baseball field which one of you is better?"

Let me (Jason) answer that question. We were both starters all four years at Liberty, so there was no doubt we could both play. But part of our story involves David getting more attention on the baseball field than me. He was drafted by the New York Mets out of high school—I was not. He was drafted again by the Mets after his junior year in college. For me, just more crickets.

Growing up, we had always been recognized together, but professional scouts differentiate with greater precision. David had fantastic skills as a catcher, a position where less talent exists. (David: Okay, I'll give you that one.) The father of Hall of Famer Johnny Bench counseled his son to play catcher because it was the shortest route to the big leagues (other than being a left-handed pitcher). So I often witnessed success in David's career that I wasn't having in my own. I was an infielder with slightly above average speed. Among family and friends who knew us well, there developed a growing sentiment of, "Poor Jason. David's been drafted twice, but Jason . . . not yet." I even had to endure a feature article in the *Dallas Morning News* that speculated how I must feel playing in my brother's shadow. (However, socially, David has always been in my shadow.)

I just kept working hard and trusting the Lord. A principle that guided me through this time was to do my best and let God do the rest. I needed to do my duty to hone my talent and let God handle the results. Having that attitude freed me from jealousy and resentment.

We like to remember the life of US president John Quincy Adams, who, once he finished his presidency, went back into Congress in order to work toward the abolishment of slavery. Every single bill he submitted along those lines got turned down—it was failure after failure. At the end of his life he was asked whether he was discouraged by the fact that he didn't see the end of slavery. He simply said, "Duty is mine. Results are God's." His job was to do what God told him to do and not to concern himself with the results.

Being results-focused tends to cause us to think strategically in our minds as opposed to spiritually in our hearts. However, when we focus on our duty (from the

heart) and not the results (in our minds), we can operate both strategically and spiritually in our duty while God handles all the results.

So I didn't concern myself with the fact that I wasn't hitting well
enough to get drafted. I worked harder than any human being alive, and
I knew that pleased the Lord. He'd handle the results.

By the end of my junior year at Liberty, I was hitting about .300,
which wasn't good enough to get drafted. I was going to need a stellar
senior season. In preparing for that crucial season, my brother and I had
a decision to make.

Most professional prospects in college play in "wooden bat" summer
leagues. There are several of them throughout the US, and they are filled
with future big leaguers. But there are also travel ministry teams filled
with future pros as well, such as Athletes in Action. The previous summer we had traveled the world playing with Athletes in Action and loved
it. We had another offer from them for the summer, but we also received
an offer from a start-up team in Torrington, Connecticut, in the New
England Collegiate Baseball League. We sat in our room at Liberty and
prayed over what we should do.

Our first thought was to choose the ministry route of Athletes in
Action again. So we called the guy from Torrington and turned down the
offer. As we hung up the phone, however, we felt like something wasn't
right. We didn't know what the problem was, so we got down on our
knees and began praying again. We both felt like God was moving our
hearts to go to Torrington instead, so we picked the phone back up and
called Torrington to accept the offer. That was one of the first times we
ever felt a physical "check" from God in both of our spirits at the same
time. God was up to something.

Two incredible things happened to me (Jason) that summer.

First, I met my future wife in Torrington. Tori was the daughter of the
chaplain for the team. Suffice it to say that outside of Jesus, Tori is the single
greatest gift God has ever brought into my life. Looking back, I understand

it was God's hand of providence that brought me to Torrington, not just for baseball but for a bride.

But something else happened that summer on the baseball field. God was going to fix my swing, but He was going to do it through our hitting coach, Greg Morhardt, a Liberty alum. A quick fact about Coach Morhardt: *Sports Illustrated* did a story on him because he was the scout who found future Hall of Fame baseball player Mike Trout (Anaheim Angels). Anyway, Mo—as we called him—had gone through the minor leagues up to AAA before being released, and he had since been doing odd jobs like being the hitting instructor for the Torrington Twisters. Not many people realized it at the time, but Coach Mo was a genius. Everyone in the baseball community knows now how incredibly "baseball smart" he is—but back then he was just another summer-league hitting coach.

Once Coach Mo got hold of me, he straightened out my swing in such a way that I immediately began seeing results at the plate. And I took the good results into my senior year at Liberty, raising my average from .300 (over three years) to .426 by the end of the regular season. I was one of the top hitters in the nation that year. That never would have happened without God's check in my spirit to go to Torrington to learn from Coach Mo.

Once again God used someone in a divine way to impact our lives for His glory. It's amazing how He continued to use people to accomplish His purposes for our lives.

OUR ONE GOAL WHEN WE SIGNED WITH LIBERTY, OUTSIDE OF GET-ting drafted, was to lead them back to an NCAA Regional Tournament. At this time Liberty had never won a single NCAA Tournament Division I game in any sport, so winning was very important to us. During our first three years at Liberty, we never made it. You had to be one of the top fifty teams in the nation, and that is no small task. So entering our senior season, we were laser focused.

We had an incredible team that year (seven players signed pro), and we won the Big South Conference, which meant we were going back to the Regionals. Jason had an even bigger year and was solely responsible for about ten of our wins through timely, game-winning hits. He was the Most Valuable Player of our team, the Player of the Year in our conference, and the primary reason our team was back in the Regionals in May 1998. We couldn't have planned it any better.

Selection day came; the name *Liberty University* hit the screen . . . and we were headed to Florida State. Game on!

Dr. Falwell beamed with pride the Sunday before the tournament as he bragged about our team from the pulpit. (He was an avid baseball fan. At our home games he would sit in the blistering heat in his suit and tie and talk with the hitters on deck. In tight games he'd say, "Benham, I'm expecting you to come through." Talk about pressure!) We really wanted to make him proud and hand him Liberty's first-ever NCAA Tournament win.

When we arrived on the campus of Florida State, the air was electric with excitement as all the big-university teams arrived: Oklahoma, Auburn, Rutgers, and others. Busloads of media and MLB scouts arrived too. The stage was set.

The first night we lost to Florida State 10–7. They were the heavy favorite to win, and, as a matter of fact, they went all the way to the World Series that year. But the next day's game against Auburn was one we'll never forget.

The game wound up going down to the wire. In the ninth inning the score was tied 2–2. If we could hold them scoreless in the top half of the ninth, we'd come to the plate with a chance to break the tie and win the game. Auburn was at bat with two outs and a runner on second base. Their next batter hit a slow-rolling ground ball to our third baseman. An easy out . . . except the ball rolled right through his legs. The only problem was that I (Jason) happened to be playing third base that day. The ball rolled so slowly that our left fielder had no chance to make a play at the plate, so the runner from second scored easily. We were down 3–2. My heart dropped to the bottom of my feet. We got the next guy out—inning over, we were up to bat.

I (Jason) knew exactly what was happening. God was setting the stage for an epic Liberty victory. I quickly did the math and realized that if we had two outs with the bases loaded, I would get a chance to hit. And, sure enough, that situation presented itself. It was like slow motion when I stepped up to the plate.

This was my chance to redeem myself for the weak error I made at the top of the inning and hand Liberty their first major win. I had lived the dream for so long and had seen God do the impossible so many times that I truly felt I was guaranteed success.

Auburn's pitcher, Colter Bean, stood atop the mound preparing to face the Big South Player of the Year. Mom and Dad and dozens of family and friends were up in the stands along with reporters, scouts, and countless cameras. I stood in the batter's box praying out loud. I could hear the catcher and the umpire talking to each other about it, but I just knew what God was going to do. I simply prayed, "It's just me and You, Lord. It's just me and You up here now." First pitch—low and outside, ball one. The tension mounted. Second pitch on its way . . . I unleashed.

What happened next is the most anticlimactic moment of my life. I hit a weak, slow-rolling ground ball to the second baseman. He scooped it up and stepped on second base. We lost. Game over. College season over. College career over. No win in the Regionals. Nothing. Just like that.

I had only made it halfway down the base line when I saw the second baseman step on second for the out, so everything inside me said to stop running. But I sprinted through first base just like I was taught. (This lesson was pivotal later in life.) After running through the bag, I could feel a huge lump start to form in my throat. I slowly walked back to the dugout. I looked around and saw all my teammates sitting down with their faces in their hands. I had let everybody down. I was the guy that had come through in the clutch for them all year, but when they needed me the most, I failed.

My instinct was to go find somewhere private and just shut down, but our sports information director came running up and said, "Hey, they want to see you in the media room. The press wants to talk to you, so get in there quick."

I changed out of my cleats and headed over. Before I walked in the door I prayed, "Lord, I promised I would give You praise in victory or in defeat. But, Holy Spirit, I need You to speak through me right now because I have no clue what I'm going to say."

When I walked in the door, I was taken aback by all the cameras and microphones. Dozens of networks were in the room—national and local media alike. I sat down with my coach and our team's pitcher for the game. The first question was aimed right at me: "Jason, tell us about that ground ball." I took a deep breath and then felt the presence of the Holy Spirit fill my heart. I said, "You know what, I booted the ball and I failed today. When my team needed me the most, I failed. But you know, Jesus Christ still loves me, and He has a plan for my life—and Jesus loves every single one of you and has a plan for your lives too. One day I'm going to have a son, and he's going to make an error in a big game. And I'll be able to put my arm around him and say, 'It's okay, buddy, because your dad made an error in the biggest game of his life, but God is still on the throne.' Long ago I promised I'd give God glory in victory *and* in defeat, and so I'm here to give Him praise today. If anyone of you in here today would want to accept Him as Savior you can do that right here, right now."

That was it. You could have heard a pin drop. Needless to say, they didn't ask me any more questions. They just stared at me like they were trying to figure what planet I came from. As I began tearing up, I walked out the door.

A bunch of our fans were gathered outside, but I didn't feel like talking to anyone. I just circled around and walked out into the empty football field behind Doak Campbell Stadium adjacent to where we were. I fell to my knees and cried out to the Lord, "Why? Lord, I know I just gave You glory in there, but this is too painful to bear." By that time I was twenty-two and had a close personal relationship with the Lord. I had walked with Him long enough to know that when you're torn up with pain and sorrow, you take it to Him directly.

After I got up off my knees, I turned around and saw my whole family standing behind me. They were there the whole time I was praying. I'll never forget that moment.

One postscript to that loss: A friend in Tallahassee called a few days later to say he was reading about me in the *Tallahassee Democrat*. He said that a liberal-leaning columnist wrote a piece about what he saw at the game and at the press conference. He talked about the Christian faith of this young baseball player who blew the game for his team but still gave praise to God. He wrote that typical athletes were quick to give God credit for helping them win a game, but he'd never seen one do it quite like this in a loss.[1] My testimony gave this columnist pause to ponder faith in Jesus a bit deeper. For a moment I realized that our loss spoke a much greater message than a win would have.

I remember calling Coach Mo the next day on a pay phone in the airport before flying back to Lynchburg. I'll never forget what he said. "You know, Jase, it looked like Jesus failed that day when He was walking up that hill with a cross on His back, but He was winning every step of the way." That's all I needed to hear. Everything made sense.

Duty is ours. Results are God's. Sometimes God allows us to achieve our dreams. Other times we have to die to them. The Lord gives and takes away—blessed be the name of the Lord (Job 1:21). We would often be reminded of these principles over the next few years as we made our next step into the pros.

SEVEN

DYING TO OUR DREAM

Minor League Baseball (1998–2001)

*Unless a grain of wheat falls into the earth and dies, it
remains alone; but if it dies, it bears much fruit.*
—John 12:24

When you let go of what's in your hand God will give
you what's in His hand. #LetItGo

LESS THAN A MONTH AFTER OUR SEASON-ENDING LOSS TO AUBURN,
we were headed into the major league draft. I (David) had already been
drafted before and felt pretty confident, but my real concern was for
Jason. Playing professional baseball was *our* dream, together. We weren't
just two athletes pushing each other every day to get to the big leagues—
it was much more than that. We were brothers, twin brothers, who had
shared a womb, shared a room, and shared a dream. It was the same
dream, connected at the heart, forged inside of us through countless
hours of work and prayer—we wanted to accomplish this dream together.
And that moment was fast approaching.

The four weeks of preparation before the draft helped ease the pain
of our loss to Auburn in the Regionals. Occasionally, while we picked up

balls after a round of batting practice, we'd talk about what it would've been like to give LU their first NCAA win, but that wasn't very constructive—it only made us mad. That dream was dead. We needed to let it go and see it as a building block for our next season of life.

The week before the draft, the air was abuzz with those who knew us, all wondering if Jason would be selected. If getting drafted was simply up to personal performance, he was a shoo-in. He was our team MVP, the Big South Conference Player of the Year, and one of the leading hitters in the nation. But there's so much more to being drafted than just having a good season.

Major league scouts look at the intangibles, despite what the stats say. They select players based on the answer to one question: "Can this kid play in the major leagues?" Period. They are looking for the five tools of baseball: speed, arm strength, hit for power, hit for average, and fielding. Did Jason have these? We'd soon find out.

THE DAY FINALLY ARRIVED ON JUNE 2, 1998, THE DAY WE HAD dreamed about our entire lives. We were in Orlando, Florida, at a pro-life event our dad was hosting. Every morning we'd leave the hotel early to get in a workout before the day's activities, and by 10 a.m. on June 2 we drove back to the hotel from the gym.

As we pulled into the parking lot, Mom and Dad were standing there smiling from ear to ear. Mom walked up to the car and said, "The Red Sox just drafted you, Docky, in the twelfth round!" (David: Mom calls me Docky and Jason Jeets. We have no idea where those names came from.) Several others walked up with congratulations—we figured Mom had already let the cat out of the bag. She just couldn't hold it in.

I was surprised the Red Sox took me. I hadn't spoken with them all season, and just a few hours before the draft, I received a phone call from the Detroit Tigers showing real interest. The Red Sox were nowhere on my radar. But as excited as I was, I couldn't celebrate until Jason was drafted.

All that day we stayed close to the phone, but no call. The pressure was too much, so the next morning (June 3) we decided to hit the gym again to get our minds off the draft.

When we pulled back into the hotel parking lot, we saw Mom running out toward our truck with the phone in her hand. Her smile lit up the sky. "Jason, you got drafted! The Baltimore Orioles! The scout just called us and really wants to talk to you."

That moment was surreal. If only we were playing the soundtrack from *The Natural*. Jason sat there, speechless. We all know that feeling of accomplishing something you've worked so hard for—it's a really good feeling. Mom said that the scout was overwhelmingly gracious on the phone about how excited he was to draft Jason. He said he had watched Jason play all year, and although he knew Jason had the skills to play in the big leagues, what really excited him was his leadership abilities. After I (Jason) talked to the scout, I jogged over to an area where I could be alone to thank the Lord. I knew God cared about my dream as much as I did, and I just wanted to spend some time alone thanking Him for making it a reality. So here we were—both drafted by Major League Baseball teams and about to embark on our childhood dream.

After signing our contracts we were told to report to mini-camp—David to Fort Myers, Florida, and Jason to Sarasota, Florida. One of our college teammates, Jason (Delly) Dellinger, lived in Fort Myers at the time, and since we had only one truck, he agreed to drive an hour north to Sarasota to pick up David.

Delly met us at Cracker Barrel off I-75 in Sarasota. After annihilating three Country Boy Breakfasts, we walked out to the truck for our good-byes. Delly could tell it was a little awkward for us to say good-bye to each other, so he went and sat in his truck. (Jason won't admit it, but I know he had a huge lump in his throat and wanted a hug with a leg wrap and a scream-cry.)

"Well, play hard," I (David) said. "Make the butterflies fly in formation when you're at the plate."

"Love you," Jason said.

"Love you too," I replied. (Jason: I don't remember this part.)

We hugged and walked away. We were heading in separate directions for the first time in our lives.

In case you wonder why players disappear for a few years after being drafted by a major league team, it's because they're being developed in the minor leagues. Sometimes players move quickly through the system while others (most, unfortunately) are left there to die. We were headed to the minor leagues with big dreams and empty pockets. (Our first-year-player salaries were $850 a month *before* taxes.)

NOW, SINCE THIS WAS THE FIRST TIME IN OUR LIVES WE WERE APART, we'll need to take turns telling our sides of the story. I (Jason), being the epitome of humility, will let David go first.

I (David) played well in Boston's system for a season and a half. As a catcher I wasn't expected to become a prolific home run hitter, so that pressure was off my back. I was simply expected to develop my raw talent behind the plate into "big league material." From what the coaches were saying, I was moving along just fine.

Of all the difficult things about being in the minor leagues, the toughest for me was adjusting to a new roommate. I went from bunking with my twin brother all of my life to sharing a room with different guys from all over the nation and even other countries, including Dominican, Cuban, and Venezuelan players who could barely speak English. At first it was really weird because we couldn't communicate. But after a while it became an incredible ministry for me. I can remember one time a young Dominican player refused to sleep on his bed. He just took the comforter and slept on the floor. He said it was because this was how he grew up. Over the years I developed a great deal of respect for these athletes.

My second season, in 1999, the Red Sox were headed to the play-offs for the first time in several years, but Bret Saberhagen—one of their starting pitchers—went down with a shoulder injury. Boston needed another pitcher with playoff experience, so they went after St. Louis

Cardinal lefty, Kent Mercker. Interestingly, during my first season in 1998 I always played well against St. Louis's minor league clubs, so they requested me as part of a two-for-one deal.

Now *that* was the craziest experience ever. I walked into the locker room having no clue I had just been traded. As I was dressing, Butch Hobson, my manager, called me into his office and told me about it. By the time I got home, my little sister, Abigail, called to tell me she saw my name on ESPN as part of a major league trade. The next day I was on a plane heading to St. Louis's A+ farm team, the Potomac Cannons in Woodbridge, Virginia. In less than twenty-four hours, my life got *flipped*.

 When we focus on being faithful to what God has given us to do in the present, we can trust He will orchestrate what He wants for us in the future. We don't have to worry about the future—we just have to be faithful in the present.

After nine games with the Cannons, I was sent to the Fall Instructional League in West Palm Beach, Florida. This is where a select number of future prospects are sent to be groomed during the off-season.

As I was putting gear in my locker on the first day of practice, a bulky athlete speaking broken English came and sat down at the locker across from me. "I'm David," I said extending my hand. "I'm Albert," he replied. We shook hands. I invited him to a Bible study I did every day thirty minutes before the team warm-up. He said he'd come.

My next memory of Albert was a few days later when we traveled to Port St. Lucie to play against the Mets. His first three plate appearances he hit three missiles in each direction off the fence for stand-up doubles. *Who is this kid?* I thought.

More than a decade later we now know him as future Hall of Famer Albert Pujols. He and I struck up a friendship, and he began attending Bible study. I can remember during major league spring training in

2001 Albert asked me to pray that he would make the team. It was the day before camp ended, the roster had not yet been set, and he and Mike Matheny (Cardinals' Gold Glove Award–winning catcher) joined me for one last Bible study.

We studied Revelation 12, which describes the spiritual battle that started in heaven and now rages on the earth. I told both of them that they had talents God wanted to use as tools in this great fight. Then I prayed for Albert, asking God to do His will in Albert's career. And what a career it's been!

NOW FOR SOME OF MY (JASON'S) STORY. AFTER MINI-CAMP IN 1998, I earned the starting spot at third base for the Bluefield Orioles in the rookie Appalachian League. It was fun to play on the same field that Hall of Famer Cal Ripken began his own playing career twenty years earlier, at shortstop in 1978.

At the end of that season, the Orioles moved me up to their Frederick Keys (A+) team—named after local native Francis Scott Key, who wrote the lyrics to "The Star Spangled Banner." The Keys played in the Carolina League, the same league David played in the following year (1999) with the Potomac Cannons. I finished that season and was sent to the Orioles' Fall Instructional League based in Lakeland, Florida. There's nothing like being cooped up in a dormitory with sixty other dudes. You would have to be a minor leaguer to understand.

I played with the Keys again at the beginning of the 1999 season and for the first part of 2000. David and I even had the chance to play against each other in the Carolina League in 2000. We didn't announce to everyone that we were twins, so the looks on some of our teammates' faces were priceless. I remember having David stand next to me during batting practice while I called over some of our players—we never said a word, we just let them stare.

But a few months into the '99 season the Orioles decided I'd be better served by switching to second base, so they sent me to their A team in the South Atlantic League, the Delmarva Shorebirds. Six games into my time there, on May 25, 1999, in a game against the Hickory Crawdads, my baseball career came to a screeching halt.

I'll never forget the night before this game—I was doing sprints in the outfield, struggling with the fact that I was moving in the opposite direction of the big leagues. I stopped sprinting and got down on my knees in center field and said, "God, thank You for letting me play the game of baseball. I pray that You get me to the big leagues, but if that's not Your will, then so be it. My career is Yours. My life is Yours." I knew my anxious thoughts were weighing me down and it was showing up on the field. I needed to give my dream back to God—I simply needed to die to it.

 We often spend life chasing success but not stopping to define it. Yet what we call the journey God calls success. As a Christian, success is not a destination—it's the journey. When you go through the trials of life and remain true to God, you are a living example of success, regardless of your destination.

The next night I was playing second base, and the guy at the plate laid down a bunt. We had a "wheel play" on, where our first and third basemen charge the ball leaving their bases empty. Our third baseman fielded the ball and threw it to me as I was covering first base. The problem was, he threw the ball up the first baseline, which forced me to dive to catch it and try to sweep a tag (this was such a dumb move on my part—I should have just let the ball go). When I dove for the ball, I left my right leg completely exposed to the runner. His knee collided with my shin dead-on, and my right leg broke in half, literally.

I suffered a "Joe Theismann" compound fracture below the knee. If you don't know what that means, google the words *Joe Theismann injury* and buckle up. It refers to the Hall of Fame NFL quarterback's career-ending, massive leg break sustained when he was tackled from behind by Lawrence Taylor of the New York Giants. *The Washington Post* dubbed Theismann's injury "The Hit That No One Who Saw It Can Ever Forget." From my own perspective—and for the few thousand fans attending the single-A game that night—the double-fracture of my leg was one of those hits.

When I looked down and saw my shin snapped in half, I knew my career was over. The game was delayed for over an hour as the ambulance came onto the field. The emergency crew gave me an IV with morphine for the pain and put an Aircast on me before sending me to the emergency room for immediate surgery. I don't remember much after that, other than my agent showing up with a Snickers bar to cheer me up and the nurses saying they were going to have to cut my pants off (sorry, Tori). When I finally woke up, I was rocking a backless hospital gown, and I still had dirt all over me from the game.

I lay there with pain in my body and even more sorrow in my heart. Twelve hours later the doctors performed a second surgery. By that time my team had packed up and traveled to another town for the next series. I was all alone.

As I lay there by myself, I remembered the prayer I had prayed the night before. Little did I know that God would take me seriously—that the very next night I would be in surgery to have my right leg put back together. God was preparing me to remember that my life was not my own, and neither was my career or my idea of success. I had already died many times to the idea of being a professional baseball player. When David was drafted twice and I wasn't, I was forced to realize that I might not make it one day. I already knew what it was like to die to my dream, to hold it loosely in my hands, but this was taking it to a whole 'nutha level!

 When God gives you something, you must hold it with an open hand. Otherwise, if He decides to remove it, He'll have to pry your fingers loose. Holding your dreams with an open hand requires that you focus on the God of the dream and *not* the dream that God gives.

At that time David and I understood our purpose was to bring glory to God by being the best professional athletes we could be. But that's impossible when you have a broken leg or are released by a team. So when God's purpose for my life changed without a moment's notice and the platform was gone, I realized I needed to focus on the only thing that would never change—the *Person* of God—and let His purposes, promises, and platforms come as He decides. My broken leg taught me a new valuable principle that I would have to stand upon years later during the HGTV situation.

 Dying to our dreams is only possible when we focus on the *Person* of God and not the *purposes*, *promises*, or *platforms* He gives us. By focusing on the Person, we sit loose to how, when, and where His purposes, promises, or platforms are given or taken from us. This gives us the ability to live powerfully for God, especially through trials.

The rest of the summer of 1999, I recovered at home with Mom and Dad in Dallas, with my leg in a full cast all the way up to my hip. Thankfully a team can't release you because of an injury, so I knew the Orioles would have me back. But I felt in my gut that things would never be the same.

WHILE JASON WAS RECOVERING FROM HIS SEASON-ENDING INJURY, I (David) seemed to be on the fast track to the majors. The next summer, in 2000, I was invited to major league spring training as a "non-roster invitee." This gave me a chance to show the Cards' front office how I would fare alongside major league talent.

When I arrived in West Palm Beach, I met General Manager Walt Jocketty and liked him immediately. I remember he came right up to me and said, "We're so glad Boston agreed to trade you to us, David. You really impressed us last year in the minors." I felt like my window of opportunity had just gotten bigger, despite the fact that the Cardinals had a strong catching prospect at AAA and a Gold Glove Award–winning catcher—Mike Matheny (now their manager)—playing for the Major League club.

That first day of spring training is something I'll never forget. Jason didn't have to report to his team's camp in Sarasota for two more weeks, so I told him to come with me. By this time his leg was almost 100 percent recovered, so he had been working out with me before he reported. When we walked into the clubhouse together, it freaked everyone out. I hadn't told anyone in major league camp that I had a twin brother, so they were shocked to see how alike we were. (Jason: For the first time David's team-mates got to see what he would look like if he were given ten extra pounds of lean muscle.)

The clubby (clubhouse manager) walked up to us and welcomed me to the big leagues. Jason and I both thought of the scene in *The Natural* when Roy Hobbs's clubby said the same thing to him. It was really cool.

He could see we were just soaking it all in, so he said, "You boys come with me." He took us behind a set of double doors and walked us into a room filled with all the Cardinals gear you could imagine. He told us to take whatever we wanted. That was a mistake—he had no idea how many family members and friends we had. We grabbed stuff like kids in a candy shop. We walked out of there looking like such rookies—it was hysterical.

When I got back to the locker room, I noticed twelve bats stacked neatly on top of my locker. As I pulled one down, I saw "David Benham" etched into the barrel. *Wow!* I thought. *I have my own baseball bat.* Jason and I each grabbed one, sniffed it, and rubbed it along our faces. Looking back on those few weeks, I realize that was as high as I would ever get. It was cool to have my little brother with me.

I broke camp that year with Potomac (A) and then was promoted up to Arkansas (AA), where I finished the 2000 season.

In 2001, I was again invited to major league spring training. As I mentioned earlier, this was the spring training when Albert Pujols earned a spot on the big league club. By the end of the first month of the season, the nation had taken notice of his prolific hitting, and he went on to win the National League Rookie of the Year Award.

People ask me what it was like to be a Christian in professional sports. Going back to the guiding principles we followed in high school and college, we sought to do two things as Christian professional athletes: be faithful in the little things and serve others. My commitment to these principles paved a way for open doors into the hearts of many players through the years.

Proverbs 16:7 says, "When a man's ways are pleasing to the LORD, / He makes even his enemies to be at peace with him." Although our *words* will not always please people when speaking God's truth, our *ways* should be pleasing to them. The way we live (or play baseball) should help, not hinder, the words of our mouths.

Sometimes, however, I bumped into people who didn't want to see Christianity no matter how pleasing my ways were. I had one coach in particular who had experienced a lot of personal family tragedy. As a result of his life's circumstances, he carried a chip on his shoulder against God and, therefore, against anyone who spoke about God. He didn't hate me personally—he simply didn't want to be reminded of things that were too painful to him.

He, as well as the rest of the guys in the clubhouse, was at peace with the way I played the game, the way I was in the locker room, and the way I treated people. But it was the words I spoke that he simply couldn't handle, specifically, words about baseball being just a game and that life was found only in Christ.

The same boiling water that hardens the egg softens the carrot. It's not the water that makes the difference—it's the substance of what's in the water. As a Christian, your life will harden some people and soften others. You don't have to worry which one it is—you just stay hot for Christ and let Him take care of the rest.

I remember calling Dad and telling him that if I kept having Bible studies (always during our own free time before a game), I felt like it may not turn out best for my career. Dad simply reminded me of Scripture: "Whoever wishes to save his life will lose it, but whoever loses his life for My sake and the gospel's will save it" (Mark 8:35). I hung up the phone and committed to follow Jesus whatever the cost. I continued the Bible studies and also tried my best to be a witness for the Lord even without words.

One of the ways the Lord allowed me to accomplish this was when I broke my nose the night before I was to be promoted up to AA Arkansas. We were facing the Salem Rockies, and I was playing catcher when the batter fouled off a ball. As I pulled my mask off, he recoiled his swing and hit me square in the face, breaking my nose. Later that night I found myself in the ER getting my nose fixed.

The next day I looked like Rocky Balboa after one of his epic fights. I had been injured before, and every time I had a choice to make: sit back and wait to be healed or serve my teammates and be a witness. By God's grace, I chose the latter, and my teammates began to take notice. One of them, an ardent opponent of my faith, came up to me and said, "Benny (a name given to me in college), I know your faith is real. I've watched what you're doing—coming in early and throwing batting practice to us even though you're hurt—and it really impresses me." And while it was not always easy nor did it come naturally, serving my teammates—especially while injured—proved to be the most powerful witness for Jesus during my entire professional career.

GROWING UP—IN LITTLE LEAGUE ALL THE WAY THROUGH COLLEGE— we would clean out the dugout after every game. It was something our dad taught us when we were young so we would understand the principle of being faithful in the little things. Seeing the effect of this on my teammates back then made it a natural way for me (Jason) to be a good witness while in pro ball.

As cheesy as this may sound, my goal was to simply be a *salty* Christian (Matthew 5:13) in the pros. That's it. Nothing fancy. My goal was to find one thing I could do that would set me apart from the other guys in a nonbaseball way. I had cleaned the dugout in high school and college, but in the pros they had a paid crew to do that, so I chose to help the clubhouse manager with his daily duties. In every town where I was, I would help with the laundry, ironing uniforms, vacuuming, and cleaning the shoes. I was inspired to do this because I'd once heard a quote that really stuck with me—"He is no fool who makes the job of someone else just a little bit easier." But I really didn't want to do this out in the open for all the guys to see, so I'd wait around until the other players left. There were plenty of nights I just wanted to go home, but I kept hearing my dad's voice saying, "Be faithful in the little and God will handle the big."

In my first season with the O's, my parents and little brother and sister came to visit me in Bluefield. After the game we were going to eat at a restaurant, but I couldn't leave until I helped our clubby, Morgan, with his postgame duties. My heart always went out to people who were willing to work hard and not ask for handouts, and Morgan was one of those people. This was his second job, so helping him was a real joy. Dad knew my routine and how I needed to wait until the other players left—so after my teammates headed out for the night, in walked my family. Mom grabbed the vacuum, Johnny and Abby started picking up clothes, and Dad straightened the equipment. That's when our minor league coordinator happened to come through the door. He looked around in total amazement, threw his hands up in the air, and said, "You have got to be kidding me! Your whole family does this too? Who are you people?" I think there were a few expletives in there as well.

It's really important to check your motives any time you want to do something for God. You will know your motive by how you respond when someone notices what you're doing—do you swell with pride or are you graced with humility? When the motive is pure, it's always graced with humility.

The next season I was fully recovered from my leg injury, but I could tell I was half a step slower than I used to be. Things just weren't the same. And baseball is such a precision sport with so many moving parts that the window of opportunity closes very quickly. An injury like mine is usually the beginning of the end as all the fundamentals of the game— throwing, hitting, and running—don't seem to click as they did before. A few months into the 2000 season, I was released. I will never forget sitting in our manager's office hearing that the Orioles didn't think I was good enough to play for them anymore. Talk about a shot to your identity! I spent the rest of that summer coaching college summer ball back in Torrington, Connecticut.

Something amazing happened later that summer involving baseball—but that's another story. For now, my baseball career was over. It was time for me to officially die to my dream, and I did as I let the game go in the summer of 2000.

AFTER MY (DAVID'S) NOSE HEALED, I WAS PROMOTED TO AA ARKANSAS in the summer of 2000. It was bittersweet because Jason had just been released before I was promoted. It felt like half of my dream was dead, even though I was now knocking on the door to the big leagues.

Although I went back to major league spring training the next season in 2001, baseball didn't feel the same anymore. Jason was out of the game and living in Atlanta, so I was carrying the dream alone. I broke camp and joined the New Haven (AA) team. I played forty-six games for them in 2001 and finished with a whopping .242 average. I decided that maybe I should hang 'em up. It was a tough decision because the dream of making it to the majors still burned inside of me. But after a few weeks of prayer and many conversations with my wife, I chose to die to the dream and walk away, despite having an offer on the table from another team.

My (Jason's) decision to walk away was kick-started with my leg fracture. Although I was released by the Orioles and received another offer to play, I chose instead to walk away from the game and got married in 2000. I had a job lined up in Atlanta working for John Maxwell's INJOY Group, and though working in a cubicle was not my dream job, it meant stable hours and time with my new bride.

When I'm asked how I knew it was time to let go of the game, I simply respond, "When the price to follow my dream was more than I was willing to pay, it was time to let it go." Idolatry—anything that impedes or impairs God's number-one position in my life—moves in pretty quickly if I'm willing to pay anything to chase my dreams. I didn't want my wife to pay for my dream by sleeping alone for weeks in a new city where she didn't know anyone. This, for me, was how I knew it was time to let the game go.

IF YOU ASK US TO BOIL DOWN ALL THE LESSONS WE LEARNED IN professional baseball to a simple word, we'd say *identity*. It was easy to get caught up in the identity of being a professional athlete. We learned that if you are defined by what you do, then your *success* or *failure* at what you do will dictate your self-worth. If you fail, then in your mind you're a failure. Yet nothing could be further from the truth. It's impossible to die to a dream when it defines you.

 One of the biggest dangers for men is to find their identities in what they *do* as opposed to who they *are*. When what you do defines you, then your career longings will naturally pull you away from God and from those He's given to your care. But as Christians we can rest in the fact that we are not defined by the jobs we hold in our hands—we are defined by the One who holds us in His hand.

It doesn't matter whether you're swinging a bat or pushing a broom-stick, who you are will never change regardless of how many times your job description does.

 We are human *beings*, not human *doings*. In Christ, we are a new creation, so *being* faithful no matter what we *do* for a living gives us the ability to live powerfully for Jesus because our identities are found in Him alone.

Heading into the next chapter of our lives was very interesting. We were both twenty-six years old, married with children, and out of base-ball. This meant we needed to provide for our budding families because we didn't make much money in the minors. How in the world were we going to do that?

EIGHT

FROM A BASEBALL BAT TO A BROOMSTICK

First Years After Baseball

He who is faithful in a very little thing is also faithful in much.
—Luke 16:10

Your *faith*fulness today determines your *fit*fulness tomorrow. *Faith* in the little proves you are *fit* for the big. #DontNeglectTheSmallStuff

A. W. TOZER ONCE SAID, "IT IS DOUBTFUL WHETHER GOD CAN BLESS a man greatly until He has hurt him deeply."[1] This seems a bit harsh, until we begin to have a greater understanding of the ways of God. He allows things that hurt to come into our lives in order to prepare us for greater effectiveness in His kingdom.

We already talked about the death of our dream of playing in the major leagues. That hurt bad, real bad, but we see how God used it to shape us as a potter shapes clay. In this chapter of our lives there was a bit more hurt coming our way, yet it was for a purpose. God was stripping away our identity as professional athletes and rebuilding us in order to produce much greater effectiveness for Him in our lives.

We've often said that when God wants to get the attention of a man He sometimes will do it through his wallet (or his work). And that's exactly what He chose to do with us. After baseball we took jobs we never imagined we'd have, doing things we never thought we'd do. We were in a brand-new stage of life, and for the first time we weren't baseball players. It was a really weird stage of life—we felt like fish out of water. We'll take turns sharing our own stories.

I (JASON) AGREED TO TAKE A POSITION AS A MINISTRY CONSULTANT for John Maxwell's INJOY Group in Atlanta, Georgia. Tori had gotten hired there as well, and we were set to begin work two weeks after we got married. As soon as we returned from the Bahamas, I would begin life as a normal working guy with a wonderful new bride beside me. However, I was not prepared for the phone call I received just days after I said "I do." While on our honeymoon, another major league team called me to say they wanted to sign me to a minor league contract. Can you say *rebirth of a dream* in SCREAM CAPS!? I was now at a crossroads.

Tori knew it had been difficult for me to die to this dream even though I had been through this process twice. But now it was back, as if God Himself placed it in my lap. She told me, "It's a lifelong dream of yours. You should go for it." I even had my boss telling me to play again (fortunately I had my college buddy Gabe Lyons as my boss). He said Tori could stay and work while he would save a job for me when I got back. It seemed like a complete no-brainer. But as I began to seek God, I didn't have peace in my heart about it. A week later, as I sat in my office cubicle at INJOY, I called the team back and declined their offer.

As tears rolled down my cheeks, I remember Tori coming up and putting her arm around me. It hurt her as much as it did me. I thought I had died to the game, but when the opportunity to play again presented itself, the dream came back to life. I learned in that moment that when I died to my dream, I needed to stay dead to it even if it landed back in my hand. For me, this meant that I had to walk away from the game once and for all. And leaving Tori behind while I was on the road was a price I wasn't willing to pay.

 When God places something in your hand, don't grab ahold of it. Let Him keep it there if He sees fit. Just like the earth has a gravitational pull that keeps things in place, so God will keep things in our hands that He wants there. We don't have to wrap our fingers around it.

I've got to be honest: going from playing professional baseball to working in the real world wasn't fun. I mean, I loved the organization I was working for and the people I was working with, but I didn't enjoy sitting in a cubicle making phone calls. All of a sudden I became an average Joe, heading off to work each day with pleated pants and a button-down shirt—not a baseball uniform. God was breaking me. Or should I say, God was "developing the leader within me"? (Sorry, I just had to throw a shout-out to Dr. Maxwell.)

The dream of playing professional baseball was truly over for me. So I had a choice to make: Would I live powerfully or live deflated? I remember that feeling of deflation when I got a call from my brother while he was inside the Cardinals clubhouse. I could hear the guys talking in the background and he told me he had just gotten out of the batting cage. I never felt more average in my life. My twin brother was still on the fast track to the big leagues while I was on the slow track making sales calls in a cubicle.

I spent a lot of time wrestling with God during those days. Finally, one morning God broke my heart as He reminded me of some lessons I had learned when I was younger—about working with all my might and being faithful wherever God put me. I repented, and from that day on I saw my situation completely different. Nothing had changed, but everything was different. I had eyes to see my situation as God saw it. And now that I could see as He saw, my mind-set changed from *Get me out of here* to *Bring on the headset!*

Our sweet spot in life is where our greatest talent and our greatest passion intersect. While this is true, we need to be careful not to see the sweet spot for our lives as simply a destination. It's also a state of being. We like to say, make your spot sweet wherever you are. No matter where your season of life finds you, you can make your spot sweet when you fix your eyes on Jesus.

Tori and I lived in Atlanta for six months while we worked at INJOY. At the time I had been working on my master's degree in counseling and hoped to eventually use it. That day came when I received a phone call from a large company just outside Charlotte, North Carolina. The owners were family friends and were strong believers, and they were looking for me to fill their corporate chaplain position. (I applaud any company that has a full-time paid position like this.) Tori and I packed up and moved to Charlotte. Within a few months I tried enticing David to move to the Charlotte area too—with a job handcrafted just for him! But I'll let him tell you about that.

AS I (DAVID) PLAYED FOR THE CARDINALS AA TEAM IN NEW HAVEN IN 2001, the desire in my heart toward baseball began to slowly change. But what didn't change was my desire to use baseball as a platform to impact people for Jesus. I didn't want to let that go, yet I sensed in my spirit that it was time to move on.

My wife, Lori, and I already had one son and were pregnant with our second boy throughout the 2001 season, so she didn't have to be convinced to leave the game. It was me who needed convincing. I just couldn't see how God would not want me to hit a home run in the bottom of the ninth in the World Series—and give all the glory to Him. Leaving the game didn't make a lot of sense to me, but things were changing in my life.

Lori delivered our second son two days after 9/11. During those days a lot of people took a sober look at life and what really mattered to them—and I felt the Lord was moving me out of baseball. By the time January 2002 rolled around, I had almost made up my mind not to play anymore.

I called my agent and said I was thinking about letting the game go. He said, "Listen, you've been to two major league spring trainings, and before you got injured, you were a developing prospect. So why don't we just put out feelers with another team?"

A few days later he called me back and told me of a minor league contract offer from the Colorado Rockies. I got off the phone and called Jason in Charlotte. I didn't realize that he had been working on a job for me ever since I started talking to him about wanting to leave baseball. Well, he found one for me, so when he answered my call, he said, "I've got a great opportunity that can bring you and your family close to us."

I barely scratched out a living in the minors—and I had a wife and two sons to support—so I needed a job if I was going to move. And the thought of working alongside my brother sounded like a decent opportunity. I was intrigued.

"What is it?" I asked.

"Well, it isn't with the company I work for. It's actually a, uh, um . . . a janitorial job at a local Christian school." (Jason: I got so much satisfaction out of that phone call!)

A janitor? The idea shocked me. I started thinking about all the janitors I knew. Nice guys I really appreciated—I mean, the world doesn't work if we don't have janitors. But me? I pictured myself in a pair of Dickies with a huge key ring hanging off my pocket. I didn't have the slightest clue how to fix anything. I felt underqualified and overqualified all at once. I had a college education and was a professional athlete, yet I didn't even know how to properly plunge a toilet.

So here I was—with two options in front of me: sign with the Rockies or be a janitor. That's a tough call. For two days my wife and I prayed about it, and the most overwhelming peace came to me about retiring from baseball. And believe it or not, I actually had the desire to be a janitor. I know it sounds crazy, and I wouldn't have believed it unless I actually experienced it myself. But Psalm 37:4 became a reality to me: "Delight yourself in the LORD; / And He will give you the desires of your heart."

 Psalm 37:4 doesn't mean we get a red Porsche if our hearts desire it. It means that if we delight in the Lord—love what He loves—then our desires begin to reflect His desires. And when this happens, we can simply follow the desires of our hearts because our desires will be properly aligned with His desires.

I had two phone calls to make. First, I called Jason back and told him I'd take the job. Second, I called my agent and told him I was out of baseball. That was an interesting call.

"What are you going to do for a job?" he asked.

"I'm moving to Charlotte, North Carolina, to be a janitor at a Christian school. And I'm really excited about it," I said.

Silence—nothing but crickets on the other line. Think of how many phone calls a sports agent gets where his client says he's declining an offer to play professional sports to take a job as a janitor! "Are you serious?" he asked. "Yes, sir. I am 100 percent serious and ready to go clean toilets," I responded. Once he realized I wasn't joking, he bade me farewell. I went from a baseball bat to a broomstick in one phone call.

IT ONLY TOOK JASON A FEW WEEKS TO PASS THROUGH THE FIRES OF his identity crisis, but for me (David) it took nearly twelve months. I guess it was because I was a janitor. At least he had a cool job working for a big company. I was in a dirty job working at a tiny Christian school. I felt like I was in the belly of a whale with seaweed wrapped around my head (a little shout-out to Jonah there).

Facebook didn't exist at the time, but even if it had, I wouldn't have listed my job for the world to see. I had *way* too much pride for that. I was twenty-six and already had several of my own baseball cards and bats with my name on them. It would've shocked old friends to find out that I was a janitor and not a professional athlete.

I remember walking down the hallway of the school while I thought back to some of my athletic accomplishments—written up in *Sports Illustrated*, all-state athlete in high school, a full scholarship to Liberty University, all-conference catcher, drafted three times to play pro baseball . . . "What's that? A kid just puked in the cafeteria? Okay, I'll be right there." Yeah, it was bad.

Reflecting on Tozer's quote about God wounding deeply those He uses greatly, I felt like I was the poster child for the wounding deeply part. Beginning in February 2002, the next twelve months of my life felt like Moses on the backside of the mountain—where God broke Him of his identity as Egyptian royalty (Exodus 3). What I realized during this time was that God not only breaks us of obvious, moral sins, but He also breaks us of hidden, inner sins—like our desire to wrap our joy around what we do instead of who we are. What I *did* for a living had become the core of my identity. And that was idolatry—professional baseball had impeded God as number one in my life.

As I continued to grasp for my identity as a professional athlete, I found myself constantly challenging the young, punk athletes. They were good kids, but I still had to show them who was boss. I'd be sweeping the gym and see some of the basketball players shooting around. I'd drop my broom and go over there and challenge them to a game. I challenged every athlete in the school to anything, anytime. It didn't matter: sprints across the gym, pull-ups, free throws—anything to prove I was still awesome. The alpha male in me was very much alive, and much like the alpha dog, I was claiming every fire hydrant within eyeshot of my new domain. It was both hysterical and pathetic at the same time.

Much of my internal struggle came to light one night as I stood at the back of a sports award ceremony at the school, wearing my janitor's shirt and sporting a couple trash bags stuffed in my back pockets. Leaning against my broomstick, I watched as all the proud parents congratulated their sons and daughters for their on-field accomplishments.

That's when it all came rushing back to me—this was where I had been just a few years before, in college, or a few years before that, in high school. Those parents had been my parents, and those kids getting recognized onstage—that had been me. Less than eight years separated me from them. That night was like having open-heart surgery.

I remembered all those banquets and the cheers of the crowds. I remembered signing my scholarship and signing autographs for fans. I remembered seeing my face on a baseball card and seeing my name on a bat. I remembered speaking in front of crowds to tell them about Jesus and about what it was like to be a professional athlete. I had enjoyed all that—and I missed the platform it gave me.

When the platform of being a Christian athlete was taken from me, everything came crashing down. My entire identity as a man was wrapped up in my pursuit of professional baseball. Although I had committed to use my talent as a tool for God's glory, when my tool was gone, I didn't know what to do. I was in the middle of an all-out identity crisis, and Jason was of little help to me. I had to get through this one on my own.

Leaning on the broomstick that night at the awards ceremony, I prayed, "God, I feel completely useless to You right now. I've served You faithfully in the past." Then I became a little upset. "I tried to be a faithful witness on the baseball field. I was vocal about my faith. I mentored other players. But in the end, I'm pushing a broom while they're swinging bats!"

I duked it out with God several times after that until one day He dropped a haymaker on me with these words: *Do you love Me? Do you love Me for who I am or just for My blessings?*

My response: "Yes, Lord, I love You."

Then be faithful in the little things, I sensed Him saying to my heart. *Be faithful right where I put you. Stop worrying about where you thought I was going to get you. You've made that an idol in your life. Just be faithful to Me.*

I had made an idol out of the promise, purpose, plan, and platform God had given me for my life. So when things worked out differently than I had envisioned, I found myself reeling, trying to find my identity.

All along my identity should've rested solely in the Person of God—not in His plan for my life.

The Lord's words broke me. I asked Him to forgive me for idolatry, for not being faithful in the little things, and for grumbling in my heart against my job.

The beauty of repentance is that the minute we confess, God is faithful to forgive us and remove the guilt of our sins. "I confessed all my sins to you / and stopped trying to hide my guilt. / I said to myself, 'I will confess my rebellion to the LORD.' / And you forgave me! All my guilt is gone" (Psalm 32:5 NLT).

Then came the *fruits* of repentance, the natural actions that were the results of my inner change. For me, I made the commitment to a laser-focused goal of bringing God glory as a janitor. It was as if God spoke directly to me and said, *David, I want you to plunge these toilets the same way you used to take batting practice. Vacuum these floors with the same fervor you had signing autographs. And paint these walls in the same meticulous way you used to put on your uniform.*

Faithfulness is proved in the ordinary. We've heard it said that God uses ordinary people to do extraordinary things, and that's true. But God also uses extraordinary people to do very ordinary things. Faithfulness to God is tested in the fires of the ordinary.

My home and college experiences had instilled in me the importance of doing everything with excellence. Just as I had witnessed the busboy at Denny's years earlier, I now had an opportunity to do the same—to do extraordinary work in an ordinary job. I had a toolbox full of principles to guide how I did my work: be faithful in little things; breathe life into your work; be a fountain not a drain; produce more in value than you take. But what I needed was not more principles—I simply needed to apply the principles I already had. My dad's old phrase of "making our theology our biography" rang true to me. This was my testing ground.

As a janitor I hadn't been doing excellent work. Sure, I was getting the job done, but for several months I had been pouting, moaning, and complaining, wondering why God put me there. Yet that day when I repented and committed to change, I began to conduct myself with Christian integrity and work from the heart. Although it didn't make sense in my head, I decided to work for Jesus as a janitor from my heart.

Working from the heart unlocks God's supernatural favor on our work. Every little thing we do—plunging toilets, washing cars, homeschooling kids, chairing the board, or hitting home runs—if done for the Lord from our hearts, will be rewarded. God will take the natural and make it supernatural only if we're willing to give our very best for Him.

For the remainder of that school year, I remained faithful to God through diligence at work. I swept, vacuumed, and plunged with joy in my heart. I had been broken, my identity had been rebuilt, and, as a result, I was now being faithful in the little things. I felt like a new man. And good thing, too, because our journey was about to get a lot more exciting.

NINE

FINDING FORECLOSURE

Discovering Our Niche

Whatever you do, do your work heartily, as
for the Lord rather than for men.
—Colossians 3:23

 If you want to enter God's rest you have to enter
God's work. The path to rest is paved through work.
#OnlyWorkersGetToRest

AFTER ONE YEAR OF BEING IN CHARLOTTE, WE FOUND OURSELVES
jobless. Imagine that. The same family-owned company that hired me
(Jason) also founded the school that hired David. Unfortunately a tragedy in the owners' family resulted in a major company split. Everything
went awry, and we landed on the wrong side (or the right side) of the
fence. Looking back, this was God's way of getting us out on our own.
What the devil means for evil God means for good. The best part about
being jobless was that now we had an opportunity to find work together.

We were twenty-seven years old and faced some big decisions. Prior
to losing our jobs, we had gotten our real estate licenses on a whim. We
knew we would be buying houses at some point and figured having a

license would save money. But we had zero intention of becoming real estate brokers, much less starting our own real estate company. For us, the only thing outside of baseball we saw ourselves doing was some type of full-time ministry. After the company split, leaving us jobless, we figured ministry was our target. So we did what we thought we were supposed to do: we created a vision statement for our new ministry, then drafted a letter to family and friends, asking for their financial support.

 When God wants to move you from one place to another, He does it through a *push* and a *pull*. There will be both a push from where you are *and* a pull to where you need to be. Often we make our decisions when we feel either a push *or* a pull, but rarely do we wait for both.

After writing the letter, we got down on our knees to pray over it. When we got up, we grabbed the letter and tore it up. We just couldn't do it. We both felt strongly that God was telling us to wait on Him and not to send the letter. This was a little confusing because we really wanted to serve the Lord and help others come to know Him, so it seemed to make sense to go this route. We wanted full-time ministry to be our new vocation, but there was a check in our spirits about *how* we were going about it. We didn't know exactly what God wanted, but we knew for sure that He didn't want us asking for money. So we parked our idea and waited.

 There are two aspects to waiting on God: the *state* of waiting and the *service* of waiting. The state of waiting involves looking and listening for God in all things and at all times—actively waiting for His lead. The service of waiting is the opportunity to serve while we wait. It's very important to engage in the service of waiting while we remain faithful in the state of waiting.

Well, there's nothing like a couple dads—each with a wife and kids at home and mouths to feed—having no clue where to go or what to do.

We knew that we needed to wait on God to lead us, yet we also knew that we needed to serve while we waited. So our first step was to look at what tools we had in our bags. We had learned that when seeking God's will in life, a person should look first into his own God-given tool bag. All we had were real estate licenses, a hard work ethic, and an overwhelming determination to feed our families. So we decided to give real estate a shot.

On two occasions when the disciples told Jesus there was a need for food, He turned and asked what *they* had to provide. In the same way, when we see needs and have needs, our first response should be to see what's in our own bags. God wants us to use the talents and tools He's put in our bags, whatever they may be. The more faithful we are with those, the more God can supernaturally bless them to meet our needs and the needs of others.

A friend of ours convinced us to hang our licenses with a local company—just to give it a shot. A few weeks later we walked in the door of Craven & Company Realtors in Concord, North Carolina. This was a well-respected, small real estate firm just north of Charlotte. We loved the company and all they stood for, but there were two problems. First, it was 100 percent commission, which meant no steady income; and second, neither of us had ever owned a house before, so how could we help someone else do it? We had two "barriers to entry" at the outset, but we hung our licenses anyway. Then we took another long look back into our bags.

We were still relatively fresh out of baseball, so we had no experience in the work world other than mowing lawns and working odd jobs in high school. So to make ends meet, we took what was in our bags and worked every odd job we could while trying to build our real estate business. It was like we were back in high school all over again.

This reminds us of a speech we heard Phil Robertson of *Duck Dynasty* make about building his multimillion-dollar business, Duck

Commander. He said that he had to fish the river while he built the duck call.[1] Fishing the river fed his family long enough for him to get his duck call business off the ground. The rest is history. We did the same thing with our business.

 Providing for your family's immediate needs while simultaneously moving toward your goals forces you to work hard and trust God—two vital components of every good man.

If we literally had to fish the river to live, we would've never made it. We grew up in the city, so hunting gear and fishing excursions were replaced by gym equipment and workout routines. But we had two things that any human being in the world can possess: a diligent work ethic and a commitment to do excellent work no matter how much or how little we got paid.

Thankfully there were a few jobs we could actually do. One of them was for a friend who owned a computer graphics company. He had recently bought a building and asked if we could stain his interior doors. Done. We made ten dollars an hour for a grand total of one hundred and eighty dollars to split. (David: An interesting tidbit here. Two years later, as God blessed us in real estate, we bought this building from our friend, and he leased space back from us. We kept one of those doors and turned it into a conference table in our new facility just to remind us of God's provision for us in the early years.)

We also met a guy who owned a printing company that needed a couple large pallets of paper stacked manually. He estimated the job would take the two of us an entire day. Done. We made eight dollars an hour. Yet we applied two principles to this job that we've carried with us our entire business career: (1) produce more in value than you take in pay, and (2) work to your ability and not your pay.

Before we started this job, we analyzed the stacks of paper and then hatched a plan we felt would allow us to cut the job in half without sacrificing quality. We were always looking for ways to systematize and streamline our work. Why take ten steps if five will get the work done just as well? If we were going to produce more in value than we took in pay, streamlining was a must.

As we planned, we knocked out the job in four hours instead of eight. We now had four hours left to do whatever we wanted. We could just sit there, wait for the boss to come back, and collect eight hours of pay for four hours of work; or we could work to our abilities and not worry about the pay. That's when we noticed the back of the warehouse was a disastrous mess. We knew this wasn't a part of the job description but would help organize the warehouse, so we analyzed our approach and attacked. Four hours later, the owner came walking back.

His jaw hit the floor. He said, "In all my years of running this company, I've never had an employee do this. Will you both work full-time for me?"

Initially this business owner needed us for only one day, but when we worked according to our God-given abilities and not according to our man-given pay, our performance changed his mind. This is the beauty of giving more in value than you take in pay; it will always open doors of opportunity. We had agreed to work for eight dollars an hour, but we delivered a twenty-dollar-an-hour job. This unlocks the power of the supernatural in the workplace and also opens the door for great ministry opportunities. Incidentally, we turned down the owner's offer and moved on to a different river—but we never forgot the lesson we learned that day.

Jesus taught His disciples, "If a soldier demands that you carry his gear for a mile, carry it two miles" (Matthew 5:41 NLT). In Jesus' time Roman law required the Jews to carry a Roman soldier's gear for up to a mile if commanded to do so. Jesus flipped their paradigm when He told them not only to carry it one mile but to carry it two. The first mile was out of obligation, but the second mile was out of love. This is one of the reasons Christianity spread like wildfire throughout the Roman Empire. Going the second mile unlocked the power of the supernatural in the early church. We can easily do the same—right in our workplace.

Going the second mile is one of the most powerful tools in business. Going the first mile fulfills your obligation, but going the second mile opens the door to share your faith. If you meet the physical need you're getting paid for, then you will have an open door to meet the spiritual need you're not getting paid for. The path to meeting spiritual needs in the marketplace is first to meet their physical needs in a supernatural way.

We strived to operate this way as athletes before we applied this principle to business. Our dad always taught us to "top it off" with everything we did. When told to run ten sprints, we had to run eleven. When told to give twenty push-ups, we'd do twenty-one. At first we did it because our dad told us to, but it soon became a habit in our lives. We applied the same principle in business where possible. The second-mile mind-set has opened incredible doors for us, including ministry opportunities in athletics and business.

Here's the interesting part of what we saw starting to happen—the more odd jobs we worked, the more entrepreneurial we discovered we were. We had always been self-starters, finding things that needed to be done and doing them without being asked. And we had a knack for streamlining jobs and doing them with greater productivity. But having families to provide for caused us to work with a greater sense of urgency and motivation. We needed a target to aim for—an end zone to move toward. We simply needed some goals. So we huddled up to figure out the least amount of money we could make in order to survive on a monthly basis—$1,500 each. This was goal number one, which we were able to accomplish fairly quick. And we wanted to earn all of this in real estate, which represented the biggest bang for our buck in terms of the time value of money.

Our second goal was simple: sell one house a month. That's it. Since we were set up as a team at Craven & Company, we shared our commission two ways: first with the company and then with each other. But even with all this splitting, we calculated that we'd need at least one sale a month to pay our family bills, which would then allow us to work less on the odd jobs and more on the real estate.

When you're struggling to make a living, there are only two practical things you can do: make more money and/or lower your expenses. We were already working hard to make more money, but lowering our expenses was even harder. This is where we had to discern between our wants and our needs. We determined what we needed and removed our wants—then we got aggressive on lowering our personal expenses.

Enter the craziest idea ever—move our families into the same house! (Jason: Please don't try this at home.) The moment we got to work cutting our living expenses, God's hand of favor became increasingly evident as we watched Him provide for our every need.

We had been living in one of the apartment complexes owned by our previous employer, and we had a few months before we had to move out. We knew we didn't have enough money to find something affordable in that amount of time, so we stepped up our prayers. I (David) will never forget praying in my living room early one morning. I literally stood on my Bible and said, "God, I'm standing on Your Word and asking You to provide for my family. Please help me get my first house." I didn't have money, so it was going to require a miracle.

The next day I got a call from Jason. "Dude. I was just in the office and heard about a $210,000 house being sold for $150,000. We should get it!" Why we would buy an investment house before we bought our first home is beyond us, but that's exactly what we did. We were entrepreneurs at the core. Fortunately for us it was 2003, so mortgages were being given to anyone that could fog a mirror. We went in on it together. We bought the house and moved both our families under the same roof—four adults and three kids under the age of five. Pan-de-mo-ni-um!

Sharing living quarters with another family—even a twin brother's—wasn't a long-term solution. But it cut our expenses almost in half, getting us to the $1,500 per month mark, and bought us enough time to keep building our business while we "fished the river." It was a step of faith we had to take.

In the months when we made more than the minimum amount—after giving 10 percent of it to the church—we put the surplus money into a business account. We disciplined ourselves to live like this for two years while we built our business, even when we started making much more money. As Dave Ramsey says, "If you live like no one else, later you can live like no one else."[2]

WE DIDN'T KNOW WHAT TO DO ON A PRACTICAL LEVEL TO MAKE MORE money in real estate, but we did know that if God wanted us in business then He would make sure to provide for us. So we committed to three things: (1) operate according to biblical principles, (2) be consistent in prayer, and (3) live purely—not mixing the ways of God with the ways of the world.

We knew that applying biblical principles in the workplace was going to be the key to our success. Our dad raised us not to be businessmen or even athletes—he raised us to be biblical thinkers. Armed with the truth of God's Word, we attacked the marketplace with every ounce of our beings, standing on nothing but the promises of God. (Can you hear that old hymn in your head?)

We truly believe Joshua 1:8 is as real to us today as it was to Joshua then: "This book of the law shall not depart from your mouth, but you shall meditate on it day and night, so that you may be careful to do according to all that is written in it; for then you will make your way prosperous, and then you will have success." Being in business allowed us to live out this scripture—to turn our theology into our biography. And we quickly realized these principles apply not just at work but in every other area of life too.

In addition, we were also desperate in prayer. We've always been early-morning guys, so we'd leave the house together and head over to the real estate office to pray before anyone would get there. Down on our knees in the break room, where the sales board hung on the wall, we'd go after God in prayer, asking for His blessing on our business, asking Him to get us to the top of the sales board for His glory. With our hands in the air and our hearts open to God, we prayed like it all depended on Him—then we got up and worked like it all depended on us.

God's ways aren't man's ways, so building a business according to how God would build a business oftentimes put us in positions that didn't make any sense. Take for example Psalm 24:4–5: "He who has clean hands and a pure heart, / Who has not lifted up his soul to falsehood / And has not sworn deceitfully. / He shall receive a blessing from the LORD." If we wanted God to bless our business, we didn't need to focus on a business plan more than on being pure in every area of life.

Many business leaders writing vision statements could save a lot of time if they remembered that the Bible says, "The pure in heart . . . shall see God" (Matthew 5:8). The word *pure*, according to the *Merriam-Webster Dictionary*, means "not mixed with anything else."[3] We knew not to mix God's ways with man's ways and to keep our focus on honoring Him in every detail of our work. So for our business, we didn't have a grand vision and strategy for what we were going to accomplish. We simply stood on God's promise that the pure in heart will see God, and when we saw Him, He would lead us where He wanted us to go.

 There's a direct connection between personal purity and professional performance. Step one of any business should be to evaluate motives and analyze improper actions or attitudes before God. Before looking at systems and process, it's best to start looking into our hearts because impurity blocks the favor of God. External favor rests in internal purity.

As we prayed for God to bless our performance, applied His principles to our business, and committed ourselves to running our business and living our lives purely, our little real estate business grew like wildfire. That's not to say we were perfect—we certainly were not—but our hearts were blameless in committing ourselves to these standards. (Just ask our wives, and they'll remind you of our imperfections.)

Initially we didn't like real estate at all. Within the first three months of hanging our licenses, we wanted to quit. At our first sales meeting forty of the best-dressed agents in Charlotte showed up talking about all their sales while we sat there like fish out of water. We finished the meeting, then went to look at a smattering of new houses listed with the company. Talking about the carpet, furniture arrangement, and curb appeal was like getting a root canal. It got even worse when they told us that we should start knocking on doors to build our sales. There wasn't a chance we were going to do that. We weren't salesmen and never intended to be, even though we were in an industry of salespeople.

None of this made sense to us, so we decided to take our issue to the Lord—we needed a niche, or we needed out.

We had heard about selling foreclosed houses, but few agents wanted to mess with the headache, and those who did were a tight-knit group who weren't too excited to let others into their niche. So we amped up our prayers and became laser-focused on begging God to open a door for us that we could not open ourselves. We prayed every single day for two straight weeks, early in the mornings in our office, trusting God to come through. We had no clue how it was going to happen, but we trusted that God would make it happen if it was His will. Then one day, as we were on call at Craven & Company, the phone rang. I (Jason) picked it up.

"Do you guys sell foreclosures? I've got three foreclosed properties in your area," the banker on the other end said. At this point I had already gotten used to God answering prayer, but this was startling how obvious He was in making this happen. I felt a swell of gratitude rush over me. "Absolutely we can sell 'em! How'd you get this number?" I replied. "Well, I called five other companies, and nobody wanted to sell these houses—they're in pretty bad shape. So I opened the yellow pages and put my finger on your real estate office." *Boom!* Tell me God doesn't answer prayer!

You talk about excitement . . . there's no way to describe it. "Send the addresses over to us, and we'll get right on it for you," I said. Then I hung up and told David what had just happened. He didn't believe me at first.

I had to promise him I was telling the truth. The very thing we prayed for—the exact same thing—God granted to us. Game on!

I want to pause the story for a moment to explain how foreclosure sales work. It's so easy even David could do it. If you own a home and don't pay your mortgage, the bank will foreclose and take your house back. It's a lengthy and grueling process that no one likes, including the bank. Banks don't want to own houses, so they find real estate agents to sell them. This is where we come in. Our responsibility is to secure the house, clean it up, manage it, and sell it. It's that simple. There are a bunch of details in between but no need to get into all those.

Back to the story. Our contact at the bank—who instantly became the most important man in the world to us at the time—faxed us the data sheets for all three properties. While the ink was still wet on the faxed data sheets, we jumped in the car and drove out to all three houses. Oh, by the way, we didn't have cell phones or digital cameras at this time either.

We had no clue what we were doing, so on the way to the houses we read the instructions: get an occupancy report within twenty-four hours, the property rekeyed within three days, and a broker price opinion (market value) within a week. Some of the stuff we read was like reading Greek, but we figured it out because if we didn't swim we were going to sink.

The first house was on Rose Avenue in Kannapolis, North Carolina. Interestingly, our first house for the HGTV show would be just a few doors down. Little did we know what would take place on Rose Avenue a decade later.

We were so excited we were shaking. It was as though we got called up to the big leagues. When we arrived at the Rose Avenue house, we realized what the guy was talking about—it was a dump! But we didn't care. Once we saw it was vacant, we broke in. I kept watch around corner of the house while David broke the doorknob. We didn't anyone thinking we were up to no good. We snapped pictures, me everything, and secured new locks on the doors. We did the sa the other houses as well. Then we headed back to the office where we completed the broker price opinions.

When we arrived back at the office and looked at the clock, two hours had passed since the phone call. We faxed everything back to the bank and waited for a response.

The phone rang. It was Frank Sinatra (just kidding—wanted to see if you're paying attention). It was the bank rep again. He had excitement in his voice that we didn't hear in the first phone call. "Boys, I just want you to know . . . I've never seen anything like this before. It normally takes an agent three days to get to me what you delivered in two hours— on three houses!"

You know the moment in every *Rocky* movie when you hear the bell, the one where he realizes he can win the fight? That's what we heard as soon as he said those words. We *knew* that if this bank—or any other bank in the United States—would send us foreclosed properties, we could dominate this niche. With our teeth gritted and fists clenched, we committed to going after every bank in the country.

We had prayed for this, and God answered our prayer. Now someone on the inside told us that we crushed it! Just like cleaning the dugout in high school and organizing the print shop warehouse, we knew we had exceeded expectations and now it could pay off in a very big way. We told the banker we would do the same thing on every house he sent us and there was no house too small or too far that we wouldn't sell for him. Over the next six months he sent us nineteen properties. The game was on, and this was how our first company got started. God's hand was all over it.

God not only gave us a niche in real estate, where we could build a commission-based business, but also helped us fish the river while we got it started. All the foreclosure houses needed little stuff done: rekeying the locks, cutting the grass, clearing out the trash, and so on. The bank required the broker to manage and cover the expenses for getting it all done. But we didn't have the money to pay someone else, so we did the work ourselves, and the bank paid us to do it! The requirements have ·hanged now, but back then, God gave us a way to build our real estate business while at the same time providing for our families' immediate needs. We were fishing the river and making the duck call at the same time. What a blessing!

Pretty soon we were showing up for sales meetings wearing T-shirts and shorts, with grass clippings in our hair and paint on our hands. We were an anomaly in our office, but the sales board didn't lie—we were rising to the top and fast. We were working, and we were at total rest.

 Work is a beautiful thing—it existed before Adam sinned. When we complete the work God has given us to do, we can experience the rest God has ordained for us. The *requirement* for work is faithfulness. The *reward* for work is rest. The *result* of work is that God is glorified.

TEN

IF YOU BUILD IT, THEY WILL COME

Growing Our Business

I am the LORD your God, who teaches you to profit,
Who leads you in the way you should go.
—ISAIAH 48:17

 The beauty of business—finding something that people say cannot be done and doing it. Then doing it again—faster, cheaper, bigger & better. #ProfitFollowsValueCreation

TWO BROTHERS, TWO WIVES, THREE KIDS UNDER THE AGE OF FIVE, and one roof—sometimes you have to do whatever it takes to make things work. In those beginning days of our real estate business, we'd rise before the sun came up and hit the ground running. We needed all the daylight we could get for those odd jobs to keep food on the table while developing our real estate business. Sharing a house together made for a simple rendezvous point. (Jason: Of course, I always had to wake up David. Nothing's changed since we were kids.)

In the first full year of selling houses and doing odd jobs, we made just enough money to feed our families, but in the second year we started to see a steady increase in business. By 2005, our real estate company began to take off.

At this time we were incorporating simple biblical principles in our work, and we watched in amazement at how these principles worked in our business and in our hearts. It wasn't the money that excited us the most—it was the ability to create and bring value in so many ways and for so many people. We saw other people being blessed by the business we were growing. Even as our business grew stronger and stronger, we still lived as small as possible as a matter of delayed gratification. We had a growing business that needed the capital.

 The principle of delayed gratification means you're willing to forgo the temporary enjoyment of something today for the permanent enjoyment of something tomorrow. The money earned in the early years of a business is "seed" money, which should always go back into the ground. Too often business owners see their initial earnings as "harvest"—and they reap it prematurely. This is why so many businesses fail in the first five years.

It was hard not touching our earnings, but we knew if we just kept ourselves on a tight budget, even when we didn't need to, it would pay off in the end. We had scratched and clawed out a living for over two years while our young families continued to grow, so the pressure to dip into our business account was incredible. To give you an idea of the pace of our business growth, within eighteen months of taking our first foreclosure property we had sixty houses in our inventory and were selling five a month. That's substantial for rookie agents. God was blessing the work of our hands, and He had led us in the way we should go (Isaiah 48:17). But with this amount of inventory, we realized we could grow so large that our real estate business would consume our every waking hour. It wasn't long before we found ourselves working all the time.

As a result, we faced an important business question. Which is more valuable: time or money? We chose time, so we began to plan for hiring other people into the business. We encourage entrepreneurs that step one in starting a business is to quantify financially how much is enough—otherwise, their lifestyles will continue to rise as their incomes rise. By quantifying how much was enough and determining that time was more valuable than money, our decision to hire others was simple. We chose to spend money on people in order to gain time. Sure, an entrepreneur could make a million dollars a year working a hundred hours a week, but what's the point in that?

As our business began to grow, we realized we were similar to social entrepreneurs. Our entrepreneurial longings were not so we could make a bunch of money for ourselves and live happy, easy lives—our entrepreneurial spirit was a gift from God so we could create sustained revenue not only for ourselves but for others as well and free up time to be with our families and give back to our city.

We learned this important business concept as we studied Ezekiel's vision of the Holy Spirit flowing from the temple of God in Ezekiel 47. The Holy Spirit—signified by water—flowed *out* from the temple and not *in*. And verse 9 says, "Life will flourish wherever this water flows" (NLT). Men fished from the river, and trees grew rich with fruit along its banks. Where the water flowed, the sea became fresh. As believers we knew that we were the temple of the Holy Spirit—so wherever we went, especially in business, we needed to be a blessing to others for God's glory. "He who believes in Me, as the Scripture said, 'From his innermost being will flow rivers of living water'" (John 7:38).

Knowing this, we found it much easier to see our business as a battleship and not a cruise ship. It had a purpose far greater than just making money. We saw our business not as a toy to make us happy but as a tool to bring God glory.

So we prayed for God to show us how to accomplish several goals through our business. First, we needed to support our families. Second, we didn't want the business to chew up all our time and leave us empty for our wives and children. Third, we longed for our business to support our ministry one day—though we had not yet realized we already were in ministry.

We prayed for God to give us the wisdom of King Solomon. We especially needed divine counsel because we had never taken any business courses. We had no business mentors and no official training. All we had was the Bible. Ever since we were twelve years old, we have been reading through it, and at age eighteen it became pretty much the only book we studied outside of class requirements. We knew the Bible was God's truth for all of life. In addition to presenting the gospel, Scripture is filled with commands and principles for living. So we looked there for wisdom to build our business. In fact, the Old Testament is jam-packed with solid business advice. We just have to be willing to dig for it.

In order to continue to grow our business without being consumed by the growth, we determined to do three things. First, we needed to start our own real estate company and not be under the umbrella of another firm. Second, we needed to increase our business task efficiency—like King Solomon's oversight in the construction of the temple, we needed to systematize and streamline the routine work of our business. Third, we needed to replicate ourselves into the lives of other people. Like the New Testament discipleship model, we needed to train other capable individuals if our business was to continue growing. This is when we began to realize that our business was very much like a ministry. But it was too early for us to articulate this yet.

Before we left the real estate firm where we were working, we asked for the owner's blessing. We didn't want to just leave, which we could've— we wanted his blessing. We knew this would be a tall order since by this time he was making some money with us. So we took it to the Lord in prayer and asked God to move the owner's heart. At first he said no and wanted to keep us. We understood that. So we gave it more time. We met again, and the result was the same. We needed God to do something because we felt strongly that we were doing the right thing. After praying and fasting, we went back into his office for a third meeting, and this time everything was different. He not only agreed to let us go, but he also gave us his blessing. We knew this was God directing his heart just as He had done to so many others in the Bible. To this day we are still close friends with him and call him from time to time seeking his advice.

Armed with the blessing from our previous company, on November 1, 2004, we opened the Benham Real Estate Group with a dream to be the number-one foreclosure real estate firm in the nation. In order to accomplish this, we would need to scale up our operation, but that would be impossible without a good system. So our first item of business was to systematize every aspect of our business.

Entrepreneurs thrive on dreaming and building systems for their businesses. Ray Kroc envisioned McDonald's as a restaurant that would make forty milkshakes in the same time and effort it took to make five. As the American lifestyle became more fast-paced in the 1950s, Kroc saw a need for cheaper-priced and quicker-produced meals, and he made these possible by streamlining his operations. He scaled their operations and continually created better systems, which led to explosive growth.

Time to *systematize*! Like Ray Kroc, we saw an opportunity to systematize the work involved in selling foreclosed properties. We wanted to be able to sell four hundred properties in the same amount of time and effort as it took to sell four. So we created a proprietary online system to organize all the steps from beginning to end. It served as the grid into which all the data were entered and managed. Any action taken for one of our properties had to run through the system. The online system also managed client relationships, phone calls, communications—everything worked through our system. It was the conveyer belt that kept everything moving toward the desired outcome.

If that doesn't seem exciting, just imagine how beautiful it is to bring order to the chaos of performing a twenty-step process . . . twenty-three thousand times in ten years! That's how many properties our company sold in a decade, and we still had enough time at the end of the day to enjoy our family. This is what our system did for us. But systems are worthless without a team to run them.

Time for *replication*! Building a team was the third part of our plan. We needed to replicate ourselves—to reproduce ourselves in others. And we didn't need to reinvent the wheel; all we had to do was simply follow Christ's example.

Jesus had a few key men He poured Himself into, training them according to His thoughts, His ways, His life. And following Christ's example, they began to replicate themselves into others—and it wasn't long before the entire world was turned upside down for Christ! Of course, we know the Holy Spirit empowered them, but the discipleship model was given to us as an example to follow by the Holy Spirit. So we asked the question: Why not grow our business using a similar model of replicating ourselves in the lives of others?

We decided to continue living off $1,500 per month in that third year—though we didn't have to—because we were socking away toward a goal of having $30,000 in our business account. We hit our goal and were amazed because we had never seen that much money in a bank account before—at least not an account with our name on it. (Jason: This reminds me of a tweet I once posted: "Faith trusts God to provide when you don't have enough money to pay, & faith waits for God to lead when you have plenty of money to pay.")

Our wives were significant blessings during this time because they supported our decision to keep our income very low. We were able to re-invest the money back into the business. Our long-term financial growth came about because of the principle of delayed gratification, which our wives fully embraced. (David: I can still remember getting into arguments with Jason about raising our salaries because things were so tight for us. I had one more kid than he did, so there were times I wanted to put the boxing gloves back on!)

When we had $30,000 seed money in our business account, we hired our first employee—our college roommate and best buddy, Tim Harrell. We provided the same discipleship training for him, which was fun because he was fresh out of pro baseball, having played six years in the Dodgers organization. Of course, he didn't know anything about real estate, but he was the right person.

First *who* then *what*. We hire according to *who* and not *what*. What people know about a job is not nearly as important as who they are. As our business grew, we looked to hire the right *who*, knowing we could easily teach them *what* to do.

Our business continued to grow, and soon we replenished our $30,000 seed money. We hired our second employee—an administrative assistant who was fresh off the mission field with no business training at all. We told her that we were going to help her develop a business solution that would enable her to one day get back on the mission field (although we did explain that business *is* a mission field). So we poured into her and showed her how biblical principles worked in business—and she flourished! Five years later she and her husband were back on the mission field overseas, with a source of revenue fueling them.

Our business began to grow even more. And that's when we sat back and realized what we were doing. In addition to bringing home the bacon for our families, we also were opening up avenues of financial prosperity for other families too—people were fishing out of our river! Business gurus call that "rainmaking." We call it the river of the Holy Spirit.

Word began to spread at our church and around the community that God's blessing appeared to be on our work, so people came to us looking for opportunities. We had plenty of hourly work to offer—tasks that earned a steady paycheck—but we also worked to get people licensed and on their feet in real estate. At least thirty people came into our business during this time, and every one of them had little to no experience in real estate. Our job was to disciple them in biblical principles of business and to train them to apply it practically in the marketplace—to make their theology become biography at work.

One of the first commands God gave Adam was to work. Work existed before sin existed. The way Adam worshiped God was to be faithful in the work God called him to do. Whether it was pruning trees, trimming shrubs, or naming animals, Adam's one responsibility was to be faithful in the work God had given him to do. God was responsible for *what* Adam's work was—Adam was responsible for *how* he did it.

The person who diligently works and understands that his work is worship to the Lord can find true rest, but the person who works so that he can make more and more money may end up rich but never able to rest. Riches without rest rot. But riches with rest rock!

Over the years we've written countless pages on the topics of business and entrepreneurship. Though we've only begun to crack the surface of all God has to say on this subject, we hope one day to write an entire book on it. We frequently get asked for an outline of our business principles—but really, biblical principles are for all of life. God doesn't segment our lives into small slices in which some principles apply, but not others. The fact that it's a principle means it applies to every area of life. Here are five simple principles we developed early in our business career:

5 KEY PRINCIPLES FOR LIFE (AND FOR BUSINESS)

1. Be faithful in little.
2. Be a fountain and not a drain.
3. Breathe life.
4. Be a producer and not a consumer.
5. Give more in value than you take in pay.

We loved being "rivers" to the thirty or so folks who came to us. We realized we had been engaged in full-time ministry all this time. We'll share more on this later, but in our business careers we were shepherding our flock (leading our workers spiritually) in the Word of God at every sales meeting. We prayed daily together, fasted together, and ministered in our city together. We wanted our company to become a tool of righteousness in our city. We were *being* the church in the marketplace, not just *going* to church on Sunday.

Our business began to skyrocket with success. We grew our listing inventory (houses for sale) to 250 properties, then 350, 450, and up to 750 listings in our little Charlotte real estate office. The National Chamber of Commerce took notice, as did the *Wall Street Journal* and other publications. Slowly, a platform was created as people began to recognize our business success.

At that point we took stock of where we were and where God wanted us to go with this. Two new challenges had emerged. First, banks started coming to us asking whether we had an office in Atlanta or Miami or Denver. We didn't, but as the requests came in, we started thinking through how we could meet the need. That's where all business ideas begin—see a need; meet a need.

Then on a trip to Dallas in 2007, we met up with an old friend who had been in ministry with our dad in the 80s. He had fourteen kids, so you can imagine the bills he paid each month just for basic necessities. He talked to us about his financial struggles, and since we had been successful for a while at this point, our first reaction was to give him money. He'd been a faithful vocational minister and pro-life advocate for years, so it seemed logical. But as we talked to him, a lightbulb went off in our heads. Our friend didn't need money—he needed an opportunity, the chance to work with his own hands to create his own sustainability, just as we had done. That's the first time we thought about franchising our business, in answer to our clients' needs and our friend's need.

We went back home to Charlotte and started outlining a franchising concept. Within a few weeks we came up with an innovative, out-of-the-box solution. We knew nobody needed the Benham brand to sell traditional real estate—we ceded that battle to RE/MAX, Keller Williams, and others. But to sell foreclosures the Benham brand went a long way, especially with banks looking to sell portfolios of foreclosed inventory. So we franchised our back office in an affiliate-based model. That is, we helped other real estate companies build a foreclosure division into their existing real estate company. This had never been done before, so pioneering this concept was exciting and terrifying at the same time.

In 2007, the foreclosure boom was just beginning, so hundreds of real estate companies across America were scrambling to get into the niche. Because we were one of the biggest shops out there, they came looking to us for help. Our idea was that we would sell them a franchise that they could plug in to their existing real estate company. We would train them on selling houses the Benham way, provide a stellar system to manage their people and processes, and market their business to banks as "Benham affiliates." It wasn't rocket science, but it worked brilliantly. Our banks were happy, and our affiliates were even happier. (Jason: David had very little to do with the original concept. Of course, it was all me.)

After coming up with our new concept, we called our friend back in Dallas and pitched the model to him—he would be our guinea pig. This would give him an opportunity . . . but would it work? The next twelve months proved we were on to something good as his business exploded. We watched with joy as he earned more money than he ever imagined and as he ministered to so many people along the way. That was franchise number one, in 2007.

The important thing to keep in mind is that we didn't set out to create a vast franchise business. Instead, we heard two cries for help at the same time, and our one solution met both needs simultaneously. The banks needed service, and our friend needed help feeding his family. We started with simply asking the question, "How can we help?"

As our franchise business expanded, we had to make sure to let God's Spirit lead us, and not selfish ambition, which was very tempting at times. Second Corinthians 5:9 taught us, "We also have as our ambition, whether at home or absent, to be pleasing to Him." We are as ambitious to be the best as the next guys, but our ambition must be to please God first—not ourselves. Otherwise, we'll make character compromises and bad decisions in order to serve our ambition. We'll become more concerned with our big name, instead of simply being faithful and meeting needs in small but meaningful ways. Ambition is a terrible leader but a great follower.

 When ambition takes the lead, the ends justify the means so that accomplishing the thing is more important than the way we accomplish it. Ambition is meant to follow and strengthen, not lead and dominate.

Another focus during this explosive time of growth was not on financial profit but on value. We wanted value to lead the way. Sure, we had to turn a profit in order to stay in business, but creating value is what leads to profit. And the only way to create value is to be a servant, just like Jesus, who "did not come to be served, but to serve" (Matthew 20:28). Our biblical foundations taught us that the root of business is the same as ministry: to serve others.

In addition, the Bible taught us to be solution providers. The Old Testament stories of Joseph providing solutions to Pharaoh and Daniel helping King Nebuchadnezzar showed us that in both cases there was an urgent need—and in both cases God's men provided solutions to meet the need. What's even more interesting is that both Joseph and Daniel removed themselves from receiving the glory so that the transaction could be between God and the king. We sought to do this same thing through our franchise model—to be solution providers for an urgent need and to remove ourselves from the transaction so that our franchisees would have an encounter with Almighty God. We simply wanted to be conduits through which God would provide for their needs. God blessed us significantly for this because we ended up receiving the same reward Joseph and Daniel did: we were elevated as the implementers of the solution we provided.

TO FINISH THE STORY OF OUR FRANCHISE, AFTER WE OPENED THE
Dallas location, we decided to spread into other cities. But we wanted to
do an experiment: we chose not to market it because we wanted to tell
people we had little to do with our success—only God would receive the
credit. We vowed that our chief marketing mechanism would be prayer.
If God wanted us to grow, then He alone would make it happen.

Although we never advertised our franchise, by the end of 2009, we
had grown to one hundred offices in thirty-five cities and were recognized
by dozens of publications for our business growth (see the list that follows). And God receives all the credit!

At that point we stopped accepting applications for new franchises
and began in 2010 opening other businesses. We realized that the same
biblical principles that worked in real estate also worked in any other
industry, so why not open more businesses?

Just in case you don't see how incredible God is in all of this—in 2010
alone we closed six thousand properties nationwide. We went from our
first house on Rose Avenue to thousands of houses sold in less than a
decade. With all that growth we received an incredible amount of publicity and awards, both local and national:

Inc. magazine—Fastest Growing Private Companies
Inc. magazine—Fastest Growing Real Estate Companies
Entrepreneur magazine—Franchise 500 List
Entrepreneur magazine—Top New Franchises
Stevie Award Finalist—Business Innovation of the Year
Stevie Award Winner—Sales Executive of the Year
Business Leader Media—Top 50 Entrepreneurs
Ernst & Young—Entrepreneurs of the Year Finalists
Wall Street Journal—Top Real Estate Professionals List (Top 10 list
   three times)

For us to take credit for building a successful business would be like
a shovel taking credit for digging a hole. We're just the tools God has

chosen to do the job. Isaiah 48:17 shows us why: "I am the LORD your God, who teaches you to profit, / Who leads you in the way you should go." As Joseph and Daniel removed themselves from receiving the praise, we, too, must remove ourselves and point directly to Almighty God, who taught us how to profit and led us in the way we should go.

ELEVEN

IF THE FOUNDATIONS
ARE DESTROYED

A Time of Testing

Those from among you will rebuild the ancient ruins;
You will raise up the age-old foundations;
And you will be called the repairer of the breach,
The restorer of the streets in which to dwell.

—Isaiah 58:12

 When the foundations are destroyed, the righteous
rebuild them! #FocusontheFoundation

RAVI ZACHARIAS HAS AN INCREDIBLE TEACHING ON THE
foundations of culture. He tells the story of when he visited the Wexner
Center for the Arts at Ohio State University. On the way to his evening
lecture, his driver stopped to show him the facility, proudly saying it was
America's first postmodernist building. He said the architect designed the
building with no particular purpose in mind. There were stairways that
went nowhere. There were pillars that supported nothing. He explained

to Dr. Zacharias that the building was designed to reflect life, which has no meaning and purpose. Dr. Zacharias wisely responded, "Did he do the same with the foundation?"[1]

Being real estate guys, we realize just how important the foundation is. Without it a house cannot stand up to the elements. So it's interesting that when Jesus ended His famous Sermon on the Mount, He did so by telling a story about foundations:

> Therefore everyone who hears these words of Mine and acts on them, may be compared to a wise man who built his house on the rock. And the rain fell, and the floods came, and the winds blew and slammed against that house; and yet it did not fall, for it had been founded on the rock. Everyone who hears these words of Mine and does not act on them, will be like a foolish man who built his house on the sand. The rain fell, and the floods came, and the winds blew and slammed against that house; and it fell—and great was its fall. (Matthew 7:24–27)

Jesus wasn't talking about houses here—He was talking about life. Without a proper foundation in life, great will be our fall. God allowed us to experience this lesson in a literal way, and He provided us with a testimony that would prepare us for what lay ahead.

AS WE NOTED IN THE PREVIOUS CHAPTER, BY THE END OF 2009, BUSI-ness magazines recognized our company as one of the fastest-growing and most innovative private companies in America. We were at the top of our game, closing six hundred properties a month. We were blowing away the competition from other small brokerage firms.

We also had begun traveling the country for consulting and speaking opportunities. People were starting to think we had something worth hearing. (David: When we go and speak, some folks have a hard time telling us apart. I simply respond, "If something strikes you as profound, it probably came from me. But if it strikes you as odd, it probably came from Jason.")

Everything seemed to be lining up for us. After all, before we ever went into business, we had dreamed of being able to speak God's Word to our generation. We thought we were going to use the platform of baseball then full-time ministry, but God had turned all that to the platform of business. Now it appeared we would be getting a chance to fulfill the deepest desire of our hearts. Here was an opportunity to step into our calling. We were ready to roll—everything was falling into place.

 Faithfulness in your career sets a proper foundation for effectiveness in your calling. Often your career paves the way for your calling. Be faithful here, and you'll be effective there.

In October 2009, we moved our company into a brand-new, twelve-thousand-square-foot facility we had built. It was much larger than we needed, but our plan was to lease out the rest of the space and use the building as an investment. Here's where it starts to get interesting. A few years prior to this, we felt strongly that God wanted us to stay out of debt with our business. God convicted us that money was His boundary for us—if we needed money, He would provide; if He didn't provide, we needed to wait. We stayed true to this conviction *until* we found the perfect location to build a new office. Our entrepreneurial ambition jumped into the driver's seat and stepped on the gas.

 God's *yes* doesn't always mean God's *go*. *Yes* is permission—*go* is a command. Wisdom waits for both a *yes* and a *go* from God before moving forward.

We knew God's favor was on our business, and we needed a new facility, so we started praying about moving. We found just the right spot and felt strongly that God was saying yes to this location. So we moved forward. The problem was though we had a *yes* from God, we didn't have His *go*. We borrowed the money and started building without giving it another thought. God allowed us to make our own decision, apart from Him.

Fast-forward three months to January 2010. We will never forget the insane amount of rain we had during this time. God was going to get our attention, and He was using rain to do it. On one of the few dry days in January, the two of us walked around the property admiring our building. To see all the business activity buzzing in the offices gave us a great deal of satisfaction. But as we walked toward the back of the building, we noticed our fence was slightly bowing. The fence was installed just six feet off the back of our building on top of a thirty-foot-high retaining wall. So if it was bowing that meant something could be wrong with the wall under the fence, but we didn't see anything that looked suspicious.

We called our contractor, who also happened to be the lowest bidder for the job (we'll never make that mistake again). He came over and said, "There's nothing wrong with your wall. And there's nothing wrong with the drainage. Don't worry. We'll just fix the fence."

A couple days later and after several more thunderstorms, our fence was bowing even more, and now the top wall blocks began to tilt. Our hearts sank. We had more than a million dollars invested in the building and a full house of good-paying tenants already in the door. The smell of new carpet and paint still hung in the air. If something happened to the wall, we were afraid the back of our building would collapse because it was built so close to the edge. With a million dollars in debt and all our liquid cash tied up in upfitting the building, we wondered if everything we had built over the years would be lost in one afternoon.

Our contractor and engineer kept telling us everything was fine, so I (David) prayed and asked the Lord to send someone new to help. We needed fresh counsel. I was sitting at a stoplight near our office praying, and I looked up and saw a man rebuilding a retaining wall at Wendy's just down the street from our office. The overabundant rain was challenging many retaining walls in our area. I drove over and asked if he could help us out. He said his boss was one of the top retaining wall experts in the state of North Carolina and would be happy to take a look. Plus, as we would discover, he also served on the board of a local crisis pregnancy center, so he knew our dad. Talk about a quick answer to prayer!

He and his engineer came over the next day. We told them we only had one rule: tell us the full truth and don't hold back anything. They confirmed our worst fears: our thirty-foot-high retaining wall was in serious trouble. Our wall's batter, an architectural term used for the angle of the wall, was headed in the wrong direction. At this point, the man said it would probably cost $700,000 to fix. I (David) was heartbroken and began crying. (Jason: As much as I want to make fun of him right now, I just can't. We were both heartbroken. Everything we had worked so hard for seemed to be crumbling under our feet.) I (David) felt like this was my fault since I had pushed so hard for this project. But Jason reminded me he had wanted it too. God's conviction slowly started to sink in.

Two days later, on February 3, 2010 (a day we'll never forget), we were walking around the building with our dad and the engineer. We climbed down to the bottom of the wall into the ravine and looked up. Dad said, "You know, boys, I think this wall might collapse." No way—it was too high, and the blocks were too big for that to happen. We all knew the wall was in trouble, so we were making plans to rebuild it, but we never imagined what was going to happen next.

After I (David) walked around to the front of the building with my dad, and Jason went inside, all of a sudden we felt a rumble like an earthquake, lasting about three seconds. "What was that?" we shouted.

Jason sprinted out of the building, screaming, "The wall fell! The wall fell!"

Dad and I (David) ran around to the back of the building and looked down where we had just been standing twenty minutes earlier. The whole wall had exploded and had fallen down the hill. The hydrostatic water pressure behind the wall had burst our huge retaining wall blocks. As we stood there in disbelief, Dad shouted, "Thank You, Jesus! We're alive." Had we still been standing down below, we would have been killed. Unfortunately I wasn't thanking the Lord—I was in shock.

As the huge cloud of dust settled, we saw that the peril was no longer our wall but our building. With the retaining wall gone, our building sat right on the edge of a cliff. If any more dirt gave way, part of our building would go down the side of the hill. We evacuated everyone out of the building immediately.

We called our insurance company and told them to come over right away. He said, "Oh, we don't cover retaining walls. It's an exemption in your policy."

What?

Then we called the original contractor. He wouldn't answer his phone. A few days later he called and said, "You'll hear from my attorney."

What?

Then we called the engineer who had certified that the wall was built to specifications. He wouldn't answer his phone either.

Outside our building, on the Lowe's parking lot, a small crowd began to assemble to watch the spectacle. One of those in attendance was the planning and zoning official for our city, and he informed us he might have to condemn our building.

We both felt like a heart attack was coming at any minute. Our wall was gone. Our building was on the verge of collapse. Our insurance company rejected us. Our contractor abandoned us. Our engineer ignored us. And now our city was condemning us—this was a wound that felt more like a deathblow.

The first thing we did was drop to our knees and cry out to God. We started with repentance and asked God to cleanse us of all impurities and to reveal our blind spots. We were both immediately convicted about going into debt despite God's warning not to do it. We confessed our ambition to the Lord and continued to search our hearts. God pointed out some other things as well, and when we made them right in our hearts, we felt the peace of God come rushing back into our souls.

Then God spoke to us a clear word: "I looked for someone that might rebuild the wall of righteousness that guards the land" (Ezekiel 22:30 NLT).

This word from the Lord was crystal clear to us, and He was giving us a biblical picture to go along with it just to drive home the point. We weren't exactly sure what it meant and how it was all supposed to work out spiritually, but we knew that our first step was to rebuild our physical wall. The spiritual component of this would come later.

So with clean consciences, our new contractor and engineer by our side, and amid a continued torrential downpour of sleet and rain, we made the emergency decision that night to bring in one thousand cubic yards of fill dirt to stabilize the remaining sheer cliff under the building. All night long, into the wee hours of the morning, one truckload after another delivered dirt for us, taking it right through the Lowe's parking lot. We had a bulldozer pushing the dirt up against building to hold it in place. More importantly, we had prayer warriors on their knees praying: "Dear God, please don't let the brothers' building fall."

After we created a dirt buttress for the building, we sprayed shotcrete (concrete used for swimming pools) over the dirt wall and dug soil nails through the shotcrete into the ground under the building to tie it all together like a zipper. We saved the building that night and were able to keep the tenants in place, but it cost us $187,000, and we still had a huge mess on our hands.

All liquid funds we had were used for the upfit of our building, and since we didn't have $187,000 lying around in a safe somewhere, we told the contractor to put us on thirty days net payable. Of course, we also had over a million in debt on the building and $40,000 in payroll every other week. We were at a loss for what to do. But since we had made things right with the Lord, we felt certain He would come through for us.

I (David) was at the building by myself early the next morning praying over the construction site. I poured out my heart to God and told Him about the impossible position we were in, as if He didn't already know. "Lord, we need money fast—can we just get a half-million-dollar loan to start? That would be so easy, and it makes so much sense. We have no choice—this wall has to be fixed!" Then, in a gentle whisper I heard God speak to my heart: *I'll pay for this. Just trust Me. Don't go into debt again.* I called Jason and told him about it, and he agreed we should obey the Lord. We already were down $187,000 and getting worse, but we put our full trust in God to obey Him whatever the cost.

Although the building was now secure, we still needed a plan for how to fix the wall. Our engineer sat us down and counted the cost for us. Because of the location of the wall, our only access for this project would be through our parking lot. This meant our tenants' parking lot would become a muddy construction zone for months. He also said the preliminary numbers were coming in between $700,000 and $1,000,000. *Gulp.*

We asked him why the wall fell in the first place, and what he said blew us away. "Boys, your wall was a fake," he said. "You might as well have put wooden beams up. Your wall looked big and strong with all those huge blocks stacked high, but it was all just waiting to come down. You had no foundation and no proper drainage. All the rain we got simply exposed the weakness of your wall. And once the wall was down, we discovered your contractor had laid the base blocks on the ground without even digging a footing for the foundation. Your wall was built on the sand, literally."

Here's what I (Jason) wrote in my journal on February 11:

Well, our wall fell. It completely collapsed! It ranks as one of the worst days of my life. Our hearts sunk to our feet. And to top that off, just yesterday the biggest tree at my house fell on my garage! The root system was totally rotted. I think the Lord is speaking to us about how incredibly important it is to have a good foundation. The wall collapsed because it was built on a poor foundation—and now we're spending hundreds of thousands of dollars to repair our foundation. The tree fell because the taproot was rotten—that's the root that acts as the main support for the entire tree. God is speaking—we're listening!

The contractor asked us if we just wanted to rebuild the damaged section of the wall. But we knew we had to rebuild the entire thing. If we were going to do it, we wanted it done right, and if we didn't build with a firm foundation, then nothing we did mattered. We trusted that God would pay for it all. So we said, "Let's rebuild it all. This time let's do it on a solid foundation."

It took almost eleven months to rebuild—two months to remove the fallen portion of the wall and deconstruct the remaining wall, and nearly three more months to build the foundation. It wasn't until the sixth month that we saw anything coming up out of the ground. We dug down twenty feet in some places just to hit bedrock for the foundation. We spent a lot more time on the foundation than we did on the visible section of the wall.

So how did we pay for all this? The pastor of the church we attended came in one day and said he wanted to help raise money for us. He said we had given to our church community and now they wanted to give back. We told him we were grateful for his kind offer, but we couldn't accept it. We didn't feel like God would bless taking money when we were able-bodied men who could work for it—with the blessing of God on our labor. We knew that God would provide through our labor, not through our begging. Sure enough, for the remainder of that year our business did the best it had ever done. We even landed two key clients we'd been prospecting for years—God gave them to us just when we needed them the most. We'd never seen so much money come in, and we'd never seen so much money go out! The total cost was over a million dollars in the course of eleven months, and we paid for it all in cash, by God's amazing grace.

In the midst of God chastening us and giving us a biblical picture about our foundation, He still protected our building from going down the hill and our business from going bankrupt. He also gave us courage and stamina to keep moving forward. We took a cue from the movie *Rocky Balboa*. In Rocky's famous speech to his son, Rocky basically told him life is tough. It will beat you down and keep you there if you let it. Life is not about how hard you're hit. It's about getting back up when you get hit and moving forward.

SHORTLY AFTER WE COMPLETED THE NEW WALL, WE GOT PELTED BY several days of hard rain again. The interesting thing was that neither of us got anxious at all. We remembered how nervous we used to get when it rained, thinking our wall was in trouble. Now, because we dug deep into the earth to lay a solid foundation and had all the proper drainage in place, when the rains came we had nothing to fear. Proverbs 3:25 came alive to us: "You need not be afraid of sudden disaster / or the destruction that comes upon the wicked" (NLT). We were built on the rock and had nothing to fear.

There are so many different word pictures this wall testimony has brought to us. In addition to the importance of building on a proper foundation, we learned that the same rain that causes growth also brings disaster to those not prepared for it. When God brings the rain, it's our responsibility to make sure we are prepared to channel it properly so it can be a blessing, not a curse. Now that our wall drainage has been done correctly, all the rain that falls on our property today gets channeled through our retention ponds that trickle into a flood plain, which feeds into a stream that turns into a river. Now we're a part of the solution and not the problem. The rain simply channels through us to nourish the earth, all because we built it right this time.

As Ravi Zacharias concludes his teaching on foundations, mentioned at the beginning of this chapter, he says, "We cannot fool with reality on the foundational level because the foundation will very quickly show you whether it can withstand the real elements as they come and invade upon the foundation."[2] Translation: The strength of the foundation is proven when it's tested by the harsh realities of life. When God sends the rain, will our foundation stand the test?

FOR EVERY SPIRITUAL TRUTH THERE IS A PHYSICAL MANIFESTATION. God revealed to us the importance of building a spiritual foundation by showing us how to do it in the physical. It cost us dearly, took a long time, and was very difficult, but now we have a foundation that will stand the test of time. We learned that when the foundations are destroyed (Psalm 11:3), the one thing we can do is to rebuild them.

TWELVE

MISSIONEERING

The Ministry of Business (Until Christ Returns)

And because he was of the same trade, he stayed with them
and they were working, for by trade they were tent-makers.
—Acts 18:3

 When the fruit of the ministry is pouring out of you, then the fuel of the minister is inside of you. It doesn't matter where you're placed or how you get paid. #BusinessIsMinistry

BY 2010, WE HAD ONE HUNDRED FRANCHISEES, NEARLY THIRTY full-time staff members, teams of contractors, and several other businesses that were getting off the ground. The tool in our bag—entrepreneurship—had brought influence into the lives of hundreds of people. Most of our days were spent developing people, mentoring and training them for success—not only in business but in life. As we led them spiritually, according to the principles of the Bible, we realized they became much more productive professionally. But we still struggled with the thought that we had gone into business and not ministry.

It was at that time we sensed God speak to our hearts, saying, *Whoever told you that you weren't in full-time ministry? You've been in ministry all this time.* Everything began to click in our minds. Back in 2003, we were rerouted into business instead of ministry, so in our minds we weren't ministers—we were businessmen. But God was reminding us of our identities as His ministers right where He had placed us. All these years we had been leading our people spiritually—much like a pastor "shepherds his flock"—and feeling guilty that we were building a business and not growing a ministry.

We then discovered something very powerful: if the fruit of the ministry was pouring out of us, then the fuel of the minister was inside of us—it didn't matter where we were placed or how we got paid. We mistakenly thought that if we didn't work at a church or a Christian nonprofit, then we weren't ministers. But that wasn't true. God began to show us that we were His ministers the moment we asked Christ into our hearts. And no matter where we were or how we got paid, we were to be on mission for God—for His glory and the good of others. Our key responsibility was to complete the work He had given us to do, right where He placed us and with the tools He gave us to do it.

Ministry, we discovered, is about passion and not position. If our motive was to glorify God, then we were in ministry whether we were closing real estate deals, mowing lawns, sweeping floors, babysitting kids, preaching sermons, or coaching a team. It wasn't how we got paid that mattered—it was who we were that made all the difference.

 How we see ourselves determines how we conduct ourselves. This is why Satan attacks Christians at the level of their identities. He knows that if we see ourselves as ministers, then we will act like ministers. He's okay with us finding our identities in our vocations, but he doesn't want us to find our identities in who we are in Christ. Once we see ourselves as ministers of God, Satan has no power to stand against us.

This revelation was so powerful for us that it shaped everything we did from this point on. Our friend Dr. Tony Evans explained this far better than we ever could. He said, "A fundamental flaw that has characterized the followers of Jesus Christ is that we have separated our careers from our worship. Many of us have not seen the kingdom connection between the God we worship, the needs of our culture, and the skills He has given us that we may already be using in our jobs. I don't think it has occurred to many Christians that God has strategically positioned them [in their current vocation] to affect their culture for Him."[1] Wow! Let that sink in.

IN 2010, WHILE WE WERE REDISCOVERING OUR TRUE IDENTITIES AS ministers of God, along with rebuilding our wall and growing our businesses, a friend tossed out a statistic we found very troubling. He said he was hearing reports that six hundred missionary families per month were leaving the mission field due to the worldwide economic recession. As hard as it was to hear that, we had no idea what *we* could do about it. The problem wasn't a lack of missionaries. The problem was the financial sustainability to keep them on the field. What could *we* do?

The more we prayed about what we could do, the more we realized we needed to do the same thing we had done time and time again in business—look in our bags to see what we had to offer. Like the young boy in John 6:9 who gave his five loaves of bread and two fish to the Lord, we just offered what we had. We were entrepreneurs who created systems and rallied people toward a common vision. Everything we had learned in our years of business equipped us in the area of financial sustainability. This is what we had in our bags, and this is what we had to offer. That's when the lightbulb went off in our heads. We had an idea!

We called it "missioneering." It would be a strategic attempt to bring together entrepreneurial business endeavors and Christian missionary work. Missioneering would be a combination of pioneering and engineering, with a heart for missions. It abandons the two-spheres mind-set that is so prevalent in the Christian community today, which believes in a division between the sacred and the secular, between vocation and missions/ministry. God had already revealed to us that our business was our ministry and that one of the fruits of this ministry was financial sustainability. Our own business had proven to be a prototype we could replicate overseas to accomplish the same objective.

The great need we saw was to make mission work self-sustainable. If we combined the element of pioneering (being willing to go into uncharted territory) with engineering (building infrastructure from the inside out) and the overall vision of missionary work for the purpose of advancing God's kingdom on earth, we could help meet this need. So that's what we did, and the result was a self-sustaining revenue engine that would train and fund indigenous nationals who could reach their own culture and beyond for Christ. Our idea was not to replace traditional missions but to strengthen it for God's glory. Our missioneering plan is far from perfect, and we're still developing the concept today, but it's definitely taking root.

We've learned that when God is doing something, it usually resonates in the hearts of other believers as well. Just as God brought Coach Littleton to guide us through high school and Dr. Alan Streett to get us to Liberty University, God brought two guys into our lives who burned with the same passion we had to help advance the kingdom of God on the earth through business: John Sears and Jacob William—these are the men God brought to us with the same vision of missioneering in the marketplace. When we say "we" in terms of missioneering, we're referring to the four of us. (Jacob is from India, and he's the only man other than our dad who can walk in our office and tell both of us to shut up and listen to him, and we obey without hesitation. John is also an entrepreneur and was born developing and implementing strategy even before he left the hospital!)

Our first missioneering company was created in 2010, while we were rebuilding our wall. We started it as a business-process outsourcing company based in the Philippines. Basically, our company does anything that requires a phone or computer—we have a large staff of trained profes-sionals to accomplish those tasks.

Our first objective was to bring real value to the city by *creating jobs* through a kingdom-minded business. We've employed hundreds of Filipinos who are grateful for the work. (On our last trip to the Philippines, we received a huge round of applause from our employees because they were all so thankful for the work. It was very humbling.) Our second objective was to *disciple our employees* at work, as well as their families at home. (In our first year of business we had seventy employees come to know the Lord. Our pastoral missioneer is a paid staff member who dis-ciples them.) Our third objective was to *engage the spiritual leaders* of the city. (We currently have more than 150 pastors and spiritual leaders meet-ing for monthly prayer, where they are encouraged and equipped by our missioneers. We have been blown away with how many pastors thank us for providing them with the opportunity to connect with other minis-ters.) Our final objective was to *support indigenous missionaries* to reach the unreached and unengaged from our company profits. (We have now reached the point where this is going to become a reality. As our sustain-ability is growing, we are about to enter the final phase of missioneering.)

All the profits stay in the Philippines and are recirculated toward these objectives and used to start new missioneering businesses. We cur-rently have two CrossFit gyms up and running now too.

So how did we start? First, we found a missionary already on the field who had the same heart to bring tangible value to his city through work. He had been in the Philippines for seven years, but his financial support was dwindling, along with his ability to influence the governing authori-ties of the city. He knew something needed to change. We shared with him our concept—it was the spark he was looking for. We funded the venture and then put him on our payroll with the task of finding a staff and location. He was all over it, and he knocked it out of the park! While he was working on all this, the four of us were back in the States drum-ming up business to send his way. We landed a couple of contracts, taught him how to deliver the service according to the clients' requirements, and he and his team of Filipinos delivered the work. A few months later we realized we were on to something.

Early on we knew that only one missioneer wouldn't be enough if we wanted to grow. So God brought us two more missioneers who served strategic positions in the company. One serves as our minister to the people (pastoral missioneer) while the other serves as our minister to the process (process missioneer). Our pastoral missioneer is responsible to spiritually guide the people, to organize discipleship, to develop community, and to help with human resources. Our process missioneer is responsible for business excellence, quality control, client retention, and customer service. Our pastoral and process missioneers work together and act as engineers (business and personnel infrastructure) while our original missioneer acts as a pioneer (finds and starts new businesses). Although our missioneers have different roles and responsibilities—with a lot of overlap—all of them are on a mission to see God's kingdom advance in their city. We've watched these three work together with incredible Christian unity that has yielded supernatural results.

We have since grown to 350 employees and have had more than 200 employees pray to receive Christ. At the same time we are servicing dozens of clients from all over the world. We've also received favor with the leaders of the city because of the amount of revenue and jobs we are generating for them. In addition, through the profits and influence of our company, our missioneers have started a sports league, a feeding program that feeds more than 120 kids each week, evangelism outreaches, disaster relief projects throughout the region, a monthly pastors' meeting, and now a budding church. And support for these programs comes from simply creating value in the marketplace.

The amazing thing is how much evangelism and discipleship end up taking place when a business is owned and run by Christians who see themselves as ministers of God. Our team has an unbelievable amount of consistent contact with people on a daily basis. It is no wonder the apostle Paul's tent business was a mission for him—he was right there, where everyone else was, in the marketplace. He got paid to meet their physical needs while simultaneously meeting their spiritual needs. Having two hours of people's time on a Sunday morning is good, but having forty hours of their time Monday through Friday takes your influence to a whole new level.

Just as our first missioneering business was beginning to take off, two of our missioneers found additional business opportunities in the city. Kevin Cracknell and Trent Pruett came to us with a concept we all loved. They wanted to open fitness facilities in the busiest parts of town. *Boom!* Now that was right up our alley.

What's great is that we were able to use the profit from our first missioneering company to fund these additional missioneering projects. We opened two CrossFit gyms in 2012. To date, our gyms are serving more than three hundred members on a daily basis. Our trainers teach that "physical training is of *some* value, but godliness has value for all things" (1 Timothy 4:8 NIV), and they get paid to teach this! Our CrossFit gyms are tools to bring the gospel of God's kingdom right into the busiest parts of the city.

As our three businesses have really taken off in the Philippines, our missioneers are gaining the respect of local media and government officials as well. Interestingly, many high-ranking officials and well-known media are members of our CrossFit gyms. It's fun to watch our missioneers and their wives receive invitations to holiday parties with cultural and political leaders. One of our guys has been featured on the cover of the city's largest magazine and was featured in the local news. They're bringing real, tangible value to their community.

Missioneering stands upon the principle of being a fountain and not a drain. We should all strive to be like a flowing river, not a stagnant pond. And, as we mentioned in chapter 10, we should be like trees along a rich riverbank, full of fruit. Christians are to experience God's transformational life *within* so that His kingdom can manifest *without*. This foundational effort allows us to make our theology—"you shall be a blessing" (Genesis 12:2) and "seek the welfare of the city" (Jeremiah 29:7)—our biography in the nation.

In the Old Testament, God's blessings for Abraham are both spiritual and economic (Genesis 12:2–3). That's not a prosperity message but simply saying that Christians can lead the way in being a blessing to other people. And one of the best ways to do this is through the avenue of work. Vocation and mission don't have to be split apart in a false division that God never intended.

Missioneering was our attempt to create something that in the long term is economically sustainable and beneficial to the kingdom. We want entrepreneurs around the world to read this chapter and say, "Hey, I can do something like that. I've always seen myself only as a businessperson, but now I realize that I'm also a minister of the gospel right where I am."

And you don't have to go overseas to be a missioneer! A good friend of ours, J. D. Gibbs—president of Joe Gibbs Racing—asked us to meet him for lunch one day to discuss what he could do to impact his city for the Lord. He wanted to provide money to a ministry that was close to his heart, but he wanted to do more than just give money—he wanted to create a stream of sustainability.

Bob Fraser in *Marketplace Christianity* said, "If money were *water*, then riches would be a *bucket* of water, and wealth a *river* of water."[2] Gathering riches to be given is one thing, but generating wealth to be given is another. Wealth is sustainable while riches are not.

We outlined the concept of missioneering to our friend, and a light-bulb went off in *his* head. We told him to take the money he wanted to donate and convert it into a wealth-generating river, which could be done by investing in a business and naming the ministry as the beneficiary. In this way he would create a dual ministry—the business itself (the employees and patrons of the business) and the funds for the other ministry. And you know what, he did it! His sandwich shop is doing very well so far.

This is how Christians can live powerfully in the world. If we see ourselves as ministers of God right where we are, then powerful transformation can occur when vocation and mission join hands. Vocation and mission were never meant to be separated. We have to abandon the old paradigm of dividing the sacred from the secular because everything God has made is sacred, and that includes our work.

Some might ask why we are polishing the brass on a sinking ship of culture and society. If it's supposed to get worse before God comes back anyway, why mess around with trying to bring God's kingdom to the earth? Well, despite all the theological differences out there, we believe God has called us to occupy until His return. *Occupy* is an offensive word—it's not defensive. It moves in and takes over. Wherever God has placed us, we are to occupy (business, government, entertainment, media, marketplace, and so forth) for God's glory and the good of others. And when Christians stand in their proper place of responsibility as ministers of God, we achieve His supernatural authority in the gates of our city.

It's time for Christian entrepreneurs to begin to recognize they are ministers of the gospel, and they can live powerfully in the marketplace advancing the kingdom of God. Our destination is *God's kingdom*, our vehicle is *God's work*, and our fuel is *God's love*.

One last thing before we close this chapter: we want to draw a distinction between a Christian business and a kingdom business. A Christian business seeks to meet needs for the glory of the Lord and to honor biblical principles in the way it operates. A kingdom business, however, is a Christian business on steroids, as it seeks to advance God's comprehensive rule over every aspect of life through the portal of business. A kingdom business is run by kingdom people who see their business as a tool of God to influence every facet of culture—people, communities, cities, and nations. What we need today is for Christian businesses to recognize their calling as kingdom businesses and to step out and start influencing culture for Christ.

Our first missioneering endeavor was our attempt to birth a kingdom business to do just this by meeting a great need for missions. Like the boy who offered up what little he had in John 6:9, we simply offered what we had—and God has multiplied it greatly to meet the needs of others. If you want to learn more about missioneering, check out Missioneer.com, or go to our website at BenhamBrothers.com/Missioneering.

TIME TO SHIFT OUR FOCUS BACK HOME TO AMERICA. OUR COUNTRY was abuzz in 2011–2012 with cultural and moral change. Just as we were finishing up our wall project, our dad called to tell us that the Democratic National Convention had chosen Charlotte as the location of their 2012 convention—the same convention where the name of God was taken out of the party's platform. Now that our business's physical foundation was rebuilt, it was time to talk about the spiritual foundation of our country.

THIRTEEN

PRAYING FOR RESTORATION

Discovering Our Role in Society

If My people who are called by My name will humble themselves,
and pray and seek My face, and turn from their wicked ways, then I
will hear from heaven, and will forgive their sin and heal their land.
—2 Chronicles 7:14 NKJV

Repentance leads to Renewal, Renewal leads to
Reformation, Reformation leads to Restoration.
#RepentanceBeforeRestoration

THE PHONE RANG AT FOUR O'CLOCK IN THE MORNING. IT WAS THE
first week of February 2011, and we were in Salt Lake City, Utah, building our business. Dad was back in Charlotte—in a time zone where
people *weren't* still trying to sleep.

"Hey, bud! Did you hear? I'm so excited. God has given our city an
awesome opportunity!" He was using that high-pitched voice he gets
when he's really excited about something.

"Dad, what are you talking about?"

"Today's news! Haven't you heard today's news? The Democratic National Convention announced they are coming to Charlotte for their 2012 convention. We've got to show up," Dad declared. "But what are we going to do? That's the question!"

I (David) knew what Dad was thinking—I can read him like a book. Whenever a huge crowd of people gathers together for a meeting, especially one of national significance, Dad believes Christians should be present in the process. What exactly that looks like is not the same for everyone and will change with the times, but a Christian's call to be salt and light never ends.

We recognized our nation's rapid spiritual and moral decline, so we knew we had to do something. If God was allowing the national (and even worldwide) political scene to descend on our city, it was for a reason.

The convention announcement came in 2010 when we were at the height of our business career. We were selling properties for all the major players in the foreclosure business, and they highly respected us. Our core set of business principles was paying off in a big way in the marketplace, so living the big life as successful entrepreneurs was appealing. But our time in the Scriptures taught us better.

Knowing now the value of a firm foundation, God taught us the value of seeing ourselves not as owners of our company but stewards of it.

 Owners have two rights: the right to possess and the right to do whatever they want with what they possess (within the law, of course). They can keep what they own or give it away—it doesn't matter because they own it. Stewards, on the other hand, have possession but no ownership rights associated with it. Even though they maintain possession, they must do with it what the owner desires, period.

So as stewards of our business and the money earned from it, we knew that during a season when we were knocking it out of the park financially—although much of it went out the door for our wall—we had to obey the Lord. The buck stopped with God, the real owner of our company and the profits derived from it.

AS WE PRAYED ABOUT WHAT TO DO, AN OVERWHELMING SENSE OF brokenness came over us. The more we sought the Lord, the more we realized the blame for our spiritual slide in America rested solely with the church—starting with us personally—even though our government was the easiest target for blame.

We love what the Reverend Dr. Martin Luther King Jr. said about this: "The church must be reminded that it is not the master or the servant of the state but rather the conscience of the state."[1] It's hard to imagine what we'd be like if our own consciences suddenly grew silent— even for a day! Enter America's spiritual decline. God convicted us that the conscience of our country had gone dark, and as a result, our culture was reaping the horrible consequences.

The beauty of God's love is that whenever we sin, He is faithful and just to forgive, if we humble ourselves and repent (1 John 1:9). This is true for individuals and for nations. It's important to understand that as individuals our judgment comes at the end of time because our souls live forever. In Christ our souls' judgment is satisfied. Yet nations are not eternal—their judgment must take place in this lifetime. So national repentance is vital when sin is prevalent in the land.

We felt God showed us it was time for national repentance, and His mechanism for this was a solemn assembly. So there you have it: the Lord was leading us to call our city to a solemn assembly. And He gave us biblical and historical proof that this was the right move at the right time in our nation's history.

Biblically, in times of national crisis, the Lord called His people to gather in a solemn assembly to confess and repent of their sins and the sins of the nation. These were times for His people to renew their covenant relationship with the Lord and return to Him in faithful love and obedience. Spiritual leaders knew the solemn assembly was a time for corporate repentance in the face of God's righteous judgments (Joel 2; 2 Chronicles 15; 20; 30; 34; Nehemiah 9; Jonah 3).

Historically, calls for solemn assemblies were very common in the United States—not just from pastors but also from presidents. More than 150 national calls to prayer and fasting have been made by our presidents or by Congress.

For example, in the face of national crisis, John Adams—the second US president—declared in 1798: "That all religious congregations do, with the deepest humility, acknowledge before God the manifold sins and transgressions with which we are justly chargeable as individuals and as a nation, beseeching Him . . . through the Redeemer of the World, freely to remit all our offenses, and to incline us by His Holy Spirit to that sincere repentance and reformation which may afford us reason to hope for His inestimable favor and heavenly benediction."[2]

We both felt we were at a spiritual crossroads as a country. And we weren't the only ones who felt this way. Billy Graham's full-page ad in national newspapers before the election that year encouraged us that what the Lord spoke to our hearts He was speaking to others as well:

> On November 6, the day before my 94th birthday, our nation will hold one of the most critical elections in my lifetime. We are at a crossroads and there are profound moral issues at stake. I strongly urge you to vote for candidates who support the biblical definition of marriage between a man and woman, protect the sanctity of life, and defend our religious freedoms. The Bible speaks clearly on these crucial issues. Please join me in praying for America, that we will turn our hearts back toward God.[3]

WE KNEW WE COULDN'T WAIT FOR OUR PRESIDENT OR CONGRESS TO declare a solemn assembly, so it was up to us to get it done. But we had plenty of hurdles to jump through.

We weren't pastors—we were just business guys. We didn't have a pulpit or a congregation. We didn't even have a newsletter or a Twitter account. How were we going to lead an event like this? This was a challenge God forced us to overcome as He had already taught us that we were His ministers, even without a pulpit. All we had to do was be willing to be used by Him.

Here's what I (Jason) wrote in my journal right before the solemn assembly, August 31, 2012:

The coolest thing about us being a part of Charlotte714 is the fact that we're not "ordained" ministers. We're not professionals. It seems like God is calling a new kind of soldier. I saw an e-mail from a friend that put it this way: "There are millions of repressed warrior Christian men in this country just waiting to be called into action. Many of these men are highly successful, financially independent, computer literate, and immensely concerned about the future of their children and grandchildren. We've got troops, lots of troops just waiting to be activated."

In light of our identity as ministers of God, we began putting together our plan. Interestingly, when the *Washington Post* heard about the event, they called and asked what church was hosting it and which pastor was leading. We simply responded, "The church of Charlotte is hosting the event, and Christians are leading it." The silence on the other end was priceless. It was the sound of a paradigm shift.

For us, this was an opportunity to be the church in our city and not just go to church, as our dad had shown us so many years ago. We realized that if church is a *destination*, then attendance was paramount, but if church is a *body*, then being the church is paramount. For us, calling a solemn assembly was simply being the church. And doing it as local businessmen and not vocational ministers, we felt, was God's way of challenging a lot of our old-school church paradigms.

With no social media presence, no congregation, and no following of any kind, we got to work . . . with nothing but a word from the Lord to act.

Well, we shouldn't say we had *nothing*—God gave us 2 Chronicles 7:14, so we called the event *Charlotte714*.

The Bible says that judgment begins in the house of the Lord (1 Peter 4:17). This call to prayer was a call for the church to repent. This wasn't to be a call for our government to repent or for conservatives to raise arms and take over government. No, this solemn assembly was a call to the church to repent, to stand in the gap as intercessors on behalf of our nation and humbly exalt Jesus in our city.

Still, there were more hurdles. As we began moving our plans forward, we were deathly afraid of a venue full of empty seats. This step of faith revealed we both had a fear of failure. We considered asking a national, big-name speaker to partner with us, someone who could draw in the crowds and put butts in the seats—just to be sure our reputation came out in one piece when this was all over. But very clearly, the Lord spoke to our hearts again: *Put down your egos and face your fears. No big-name speakers. Be locally led. This cannot be another cool ministry event. Call My people to get on their faces before Me and cry out in repentance—start there first. And don't do it in a church building—do it in public, the day before the convention.*

What? No big names to draw a crowd? No church building? The day before the convention? Seriously? We knew this event could be characterized as another political rant, which it wasn't, but to do it the day before the convention in the public square? We were not only starting from nothing, but we were starting in the negative. We could feel the panic attacks coming on—we had to face our fear of failure head-on and host this event in an unconventional way. But deep in our guts we had a conviction to do what God had called us to do, whatever the cost.

SOME SAY THAT CHARLOTTE IS THE "LUKEWARM CORRIDOR" OF THE South. We have something like thirteen hundred churches in the metro area, probably one of the highest per capita rates in the world. We have a church on nearly every corner of the city, yet when was the last time our churches united for the sake of God's glory?

Moreover, how were churches in our city—and nation—growing at breakneck speed while the culture surrounding them was dying at the same speed? Had the "salt of the earth" (Matthew 5:13) lost its saltiness?

With all this running through our heads, we began calling around to area pastors. We told them our plans and asked for their support. We even asked if some of them wanted to lead it. Early on, many pastors turned away. It sounded too political for them. But our event wasn't political—it was a spiritual call to a solemn assembly. We assured them that we'd do the same thing if it was the Republicans who had come to town or the Olympics—that there was nothing about our event that came about strictly in response to the Democratic Party. We simply said the eyes of the nation were going to be on our city, and we as the united churches of Charlotte needed to be a public witness for Jesus. Sadly, many spiritual leaders declined our invitation. We realized how polarized and powerless the church had become.

Another hurdle was the considerable risk for our business. We had some long conversations about the possibility of losing business by identifying ourselves openly as Christians and boldly calling for repentance. Would some of our major governmental and banking partners suddenly find reason to take their business elsewhere? The fact that many pastors ran the other way certainly made us think twice about the decision to lead this event. But we prayed about it and read Mark 8:35: "Whoever wishes to save his life will lose it, but whoever loses his life for My sake and the gospel's will save it." We decided that whatever the cost to our business we were moving forward.

As the venue for the event, we chose the ten-thousand-seat Verizon Wireless Amphitheater (now PNC Music Pavilion), a major concert venue in Charlotte. By having it there, we would be out from under the shadow of the church building and in the public square for the world to see. But this place was going to cost big bucks. We were faced with yet another decision.

The typical way we had seen ministry events like this done in the past was to raise money. But after prayer we knew we couldn't do that. God had put this event in our hearts, and He was going to give us the money to pay for it. He told us to put *His* money where *our* mouths were. So we decided to pay for it ourselves. We still remember seeing the contract for the amphitheater: all the crooked numbers and the big, fat comma in the middle made us nauseous.

Everything was now in place, so we put together a website, began posting blogs each morning, started a Facebook page, and turned up the frequency of calls to pastors. We really desired for the spiritual fathers in the city to lead the prayer, the music, and the preaching. At a bare minimum we figured that we needed to get about fifteen pastors in place to lead. We prayed and sought counsel from those closest to us, and we came up with a list. We cast the vision to these people. We reminded them of their responsibility as spiritual leaders of the city and assured them that we didn't want their money and that this wasn't a political rant. Within a few weeks we had all of them—across denominational lines.

It helped that our business had a good reputation in the city as well, by God's grace and despite the two of us. These pastors knew we weren't fly-by-night guys, coming into town just to host an event and leave the next day. They knew we loved our city and had skin in the game of leading and serving in our community. Plus, they liked the fact we weren't asking for money or building our own brand around the event.

Our first meeting together was in the parking lot at First Baptist Church of Charlotte—many for the first time together. (Jason: We showed up in workout clothes and dripping sweat from a workout we had just completed in the park next to the church. It was funny to see the look on some of the pastors' faces. We got our sweat on before we got our pray on!)

We talked about the condition of our nation and the responsibility each of us had in leading this solemn assembly. Together, our hearts were heavy, and our eyes were wet with tears. Some of these pastors were under pressure from their congregations not to be involved in any way, yet they chose to participate, whatever the cost. Then we prayed together for the first time, and we knew at that moment that God's hand was on this. To see fifteen pastors on their knees and faces in the parking lot, weeping before the Lord, crying out to God in repentance and for awakening in America, was a powerful picture.

Over the next six months we hosted dozens of meetings, bringing more and more leaders into the circle of prayer and seeking God's face together. We added seventy pastors pretty quickly, probably because we hosted one meeting at a Brazilian steakhouse and 150 leaders showed up. Feed them steak, and they will come!

Even without the support of 80 percent of the Charlotte churches—unfortunately, participating in a solemn assembly the night before the DNC was too controversial for several pastors—the momentum began to build. To those who chose not to be involved, we simply responded in love. But a point we must make here is that lucrative book deals and immense church budgets shouldn't cause a Christian's influence to dwindle in the nation. Christians can be both winsome and forthright—full of both truth and love.

 Truth is a Person, and love is the same Person, whose name is Jesus. To be either one or the other is to divide Christ. Love without truth is not biblical love, and truth without love is not biblical truth. More importantly, one without the other is not Jesus. We *can* and *should be* both.

By this time the *Charlotte Observer* and other newspapers had picked up on some of our regional meetings and taken notice of the forthcoming event. The spin was that a bunch of Christians were gathering the night before the DNC in order to demonstrate and protest. Using those words, of course, creates a misleading narrative. We realized that creating false narratives is one of Satan's go-to moves, but they're easy to overcome once we decide to follow Jesus no matter what the cost.

But we knew that perception is not reality, and we had to abandon the idea that we can keep the world from characterizing us wrongly. Jesus said in Matthew 5:11 that we would be falsely accused, and David said in Psalm 56:5 that his enemies twist his words. So we're in good company when the media tries to twist our words and falsely accuse us. We cannot live freely in obedience to God as long as we are overly concerned with the world having a positive perception of us.

Concerning ourselves with perception (what people say about us) makes man-pleasers. Concerning ourselves with reality (what God says about us) makes God-pleasers. We must not concern ourselves with the lies or the applause of man but only with what God says is true. Perception is not reality—reality is reality.

IN THE MONTHS LEADING UP TO THE SOLEMN ASSEMBLY, WE REALized there were additional opportunities for the church to make an impact in the city of Charlotte during the DNC. A grievous fact about our nation's moral condition is that whenever a major event comes to a city, there will inevitably be a spike in human trafficking. So we decided to partner with our friends at The Justice Project to fight this evil. Often the victims involved are held captive, and the only time they're alone is when they visit the bathroom. So we placed in hotel bathrooms bars of soap that had a toll-free number to a national hotline they could call for help. The call center had a "heat map" showing where calls were coming from at a certain time, and during the week of the convention the city of Charlotte was lighting it up. That alone should drive the church to its knees in every city across America.

A second opportunity we had—or almost had—was the distribution of gift baskets to all the delegates to the convention. We knew that more than fifteen hundred delegates would be coming to our city, many with their families. As a show of hospitality and Christian love, we wanted to give each of them a gift basket—full of local North Carolina items—and offer our services to them if they needed anything, such as transportation, child care, medical help, or prayer. We had thirty-five churches partnered with us to make the delegates feel at home in Charlotte.

We called the DNC for approval—no. We called the mayor for approval—no. The mayor pro tem actually liked the idea and batted it back up the line to the host committee—no. So we decided to approach the individual hotels and ask them to deliver the baskets upon the delegates' arrival, but the hotels said it was too political. Gift baskets . . . political? This was the first time we had seen polarization so thick that people wouldn't even accept Southern hospitality from churches. They weren't saying no because of what we were giving them—they were saying no because of who we were.

THE NIGHT FINALLY CAME, AND IT WAS POWERFUL—A REAL MOVE OF the Lord among His people. Nine thousand people showed up from approximately 150 churches. We were overwhelmed with the response from the church of Charlotte and were incredibly encouraged that God is alive and well among His people, especially those whose hearts are humble and repentant before Him. In video clips of the event, you can see it for yourself.[4] One night produced so much spiritual fruit.

Observers noted the racial diversity of the event. Our pastoral team consisted of Korean, Hispanic, African American, and Caucasian leaders. And without a doubt, two of the best speakers were our African American brothers. Billy Graham, a native of Charlotte, once famously said, "The most segregated hour of the week in America is the eleven o'clock Sunday morning Christian church service."[5] For at least a few hours in Charlotte, that was not the case.

People were greatly encouraged throughout the night but probably none more than the pastors who attended. We called all the pastors to the altar and asked the crowd to pray for them—and the place erupted in prayer. Then we asked each of the pastors to turn and pray for the other pastors around them the very same things for their ministries that they had been praying for themselves. There wasn't a dry eye in the place.

You've got to check out the video—four minutes of your time is well worth the investment.[6] These men had not prayed with that many of their fellow local pastors in a long time—or ever! We had front-row seats to see God start to move among His leaders (shepherds) in our own backyard.

By the end of it all, we had facilitated a citywide prayer service of repentance when the eyes of our nation were on our city—the day before the DNC opened. We don't say that for our own glory (Matthew 6:3). We're not the only businessmen God has chosen to step into their ministerial calling for His glory in a city. But we hope our testimony puts a spark of fire into the hearts of others to do what God tells them—whatever the cost.

One of the highlights of the night was seeing nine thousand people sign the "Declaration of National Spiritual Emergency." We teamed up with our friends at OneCry to customize this document for the event. It expressed our belief that the sins of America found their roots in the church, and, as a result, the church has pulled out and retreated from the gates of the city. Here is the statement:

DECLARATION OF NATIONAL SPIRITUAL EMERGENCY

With heavy hearts, we recognize that the church in America is in a state of spiritual emergency. Like the churches warned in Revelation, we have become lukewarm and compromised, and the light of our witness has grown dim.

We confess that despite access to more resources and biblical teaching than any other group of believers in history, we are not characterized by the supernatural power of the Holy Spirit. And we acknowledge our lack of widespread impact for Christ on our lost and disintegrating culture.

But God is waking us from our slumber and mobilizing us to pray earnestly for revival. Together, we desire to travel the narrow road of brokenness, humility, and repentance.

In desperation for God, we cry out for the extraordinary work of the Holy Spirit in our day. We believe that true revival is the only hope to reverse our spiritual recession and enable us once again to display the beauty of Jesus Christ and His gospel throughout the world.

Because we believe that only Christ can save, heal, and revive, we pledge to:

TURN—in humble repentance from every sin God reveals to us
PRAY—with urgency for spiritual recovery and awakening
UNITE—with other believers in spreading the hope of Christ-centered revival
SHARE—the truth in love no matter the cost

HISTORY IS NOT JUST *CHRONOLOGY*—KNOWING ALL THE FACTS. History is *His* story—knowing *why* the facts are the facts. The Democratic National Convention came to our hometown in September 2012, and that's a fact. But *why* it came to our city . . . the answer had a lot to do with returning to our biblical, historical foundation through prayer and repentance. Though most Americans didn't see it, God did. And God always blesses the faithfulness of His remnant. One hundred fifty pastors in Charlotte would agree.

FOURTEEN

BREATHE LIFE INTO YOUR CITY

The Result of Reformation

Seek the welfare of the city where I have sent you into exile, and pray to the LORD on its behalf; for in its welfare you will have welfare.
—Jeremiah 29:7

 True profit is not defined as financial gain, but that which leads to life. #BringProfit #BreatheLIFE

AS WE SET OUR MINDS TO HONOR THE LORD THROUGH CHARLOTTE714—despite fears that our company could suffer as a result—quite the opposite happened in our business.

Here's what I (Jason) wrote in my journal on September 3, 2012:

Our first day back in the office after C714 we received 10 property assignments—this has to be a new record for us! It is as if God is saying, "If you honor Me, I will honor you—if you handle My business I will handle yours."

141

We also began to see an increasing platform of influence given to us. An increase in our media exposure and more ministry opportunities in the city combined to set the stage for everything that follows in the final chapters of our story in this book.

Over the few days following the solemn assembly, we received dozens of phone calls from national press and local pastors. The media coverage and pastoral feedback were very encouraging. As a matter of fact, Charlotte pastors kept our phone ringing. They were pumped about all that had taken place at Charlotte714. After all the months of preparation, we were thankful to hear how much the event had encouraged the local church.

But with the event finished, people began to ask, "Can we do another one?" and "What other things should we do?" Great questions! We told them to remember the lessons of Nehemiah 4:15–17. Take your place on the wall with a trowel in one hand and a sword in the other. Pick up your trowel and be faithful in your work, whatever that may be. And keep your sword sharp for the spiritual fight that comes through the exposed places in the wall.

Okay, some of that Bible story might have flown right past you just now. We know that not everyone had a dad who parked himself in front of the Bible every single morning and made sure we did too. But the gist of the story is that Nehemiah was a leader of the people who had a task to complete and an enemy to defeat. The task was to rebuild the walls of Jerusalem (for walls, you need a trowel). The enemies were those who didn't want the wall to be rebuilt (for enemies, you need a sword). Historically, when walls were broken down around a city, it created exposed places where enemies had easy access to steal, kill, and destroy (John 10:10). Nehemiah took his place on the wall with a trowel in one hand and a sword in the other.

For everyone looking to us for leadership, we told them to get busy with their trowels, seeking the good of the city, but also to be ready with their swords to fight the spiritual battles at the exposed places. Soon we'll explain our involvement at the exposed places in the wall of our city.

But first we need to talk briefly about one thing that happened at the

Democratic National Convention that caught the attention of America. When the DNC opened, in moves that weren't without controversy even within their own party, the delegates eliminated any reference to God in the party platform. Further, they removed reference to Jerusalem as being the capital of Israel.

Major media outlets may not have been overly concerned with the theological implications of this platform revision, but they wanted to get informed analysis from people on both sides of the issue. We had just flown to Dallas for a business meeting. *Fox and Friends* was in Charlotte covering the convention, and they called our company for a comment from us. Now, why would Fox News call the Benham Real Estate Group when they wanted a comment on what the evangelical community thinks about what happened at the DNC? I assure you, if they were looking for the most informed, scholarly opinion, they wouldn't have called us! And they certainly weren't looking for the coolest evangelical leaders or ones who had the largest churches. They were simply looking for Christians who were speaking about what was going on.

Now, we know exactly how cowardly and without conviction we've been many times in our lives—more than we care to remember. But during Charlotte714 God graciously gave us the courage to stand in our place of responsibility as the salt and light (Matthew 5:13–16). We learned as young men that if you reject this responsibility, you lose your authority. We've seen this in marriage, the workplace, and also in the church. So we knew that during Charlotte714, God was calling us to stand in our place of responsibility, which was on our faces in humble repentance and intercession. As a result, God gave us authority to speak to the issues of the day.

To this point, we love what the Reverend Dr. Martin Luther King Jr. said: "If the church does not recapture its prophetic zeal, it will become an irrelevant social club without moral or spiritual authority."[1]

 Authority follows responsibility. The way to receive authority is to stand in your proper place of responsibility. If you abandon your responsibility, you forfeit your authority. Consider fatherlessness in America—when men forsake their responsibility in the home, they lose authority in culture. Evil gains authority in a nation when men refuse to stand in their place of responsibility in the home.

So we gave *Fox and Friends* our comment from Judges 5:8: "They chose new gods; / Then there was war in the gates" (NKJV). They didn't publish our comments, which didn't surprise us, but it was interesting that they would call a couple real estate dudes in the first place for a comment about the DNC's revised platform. Another paradigm shift was taking root.

While we were still in Dallas on business, Christian talk radio host Janet Mefferd called and asked to interview one of us on her program. (Jason: David has always been the more vocal one, so I let him take this call.)

This interview took place on Wednesday, September 5, 2012, the same day that controversy broke out on the floor of the DNC among delegates about recent changes in their platform. In the midst of all the media storm over the DNC, I (David) went on-air with Mefferd and discussed how the church needs to repent. I remained true to the message of Charlotte714 and said:

> We will always finger-point, but we don't realize that if 87 percent of Americans are "Christians" and yet we have abortion on demand; we have no-fault divorce; we have pornography and perversion; we have homosexuality and its agenda that is attacking the nation; we have adultery; we have all of these things; we even have allowed demonic ideologies to take our universities and our public school systems while the church sits silent and just builds big churches. We are so complacent, we are so apathetic, and we are very hypocritical in the church. That's why the Bible says judgment begins in the house of God. So when we prayed at 714 we asked God, and our city, to forgive us for allowing these things in the house of God.[2]

Mefferd understood exactly what I said and gave hearty assent.

The next day (Thursday, September 6), a website called Right Wing Watch published a blog post about the Mefferd interview and Charlotte714. We had never heard of this website before. But the article was the first time we had been publicly labeled as haters, so it's important we mention them. God knows how cowardly we can be as believers, so I guess He used Right Wing Watch to ensure the two of us had nowhere to hide.

The post on the website was titled, "Charlotte Prayer Rally Repents for 'Homosexuality and its Agenda that is Attacking the Nation.'"[3] We didn't even see it when it first came out. When we finally did read the article, it didn't seem like a big deal. Folks are entitled to their opinions, and honestly, the article didn't give much analysis anyway—half of it consisted of transcriptions from the previous day's interview with Mefferd. In other words, it was mostly our own words—so it had little effect. We dodged the bullet . . . or so we thought.

One thing the article did do, however, was turn the media world on to the traditional Christian values of the Benham brothers—and turn those values into "anti-" positions. It was very effective in that regard, and for that we felt honored to be slandered and mischaracterized as Christ said would happen when we stand for Him (John 15:20).

REMEMBER EARLIER IN THIS CHAPTER, WE TOLD OUR CHRISTIAN friends in Charlotte to pick up their trowels and swords and get busy seeking the good of the city. An interesting point is that our trowel, which is our God-given tool for work, can also be used as our sword to fight God's battles.

A good example of this is found in Judges 3:31 in the life of Shamgar. (Want to name your next child Shamgar?) There is only one verse written about him in the Bible, but it's packed with an incredible truth. He "struck down six hundred Philistines with an oxgoad; and he also saved Israel."

His oxgoad? This was a long pole used by farmers to prod sluggish oxen while plowing their fields. Because of the agrarian nature of Israel, Shamgar was more than likely a farmer who used an oxgoad as a tool for work. What's interesting is that he took the same tool he used for work and used it as a weapon to bring life to others and defeat God's enemies! We can do the same, just like Shamgar.

For us, our trowel (or oxgoad) at this time was a real estate business specializing in foreclosures that could be replicated in cities across America. This required a clear vision, a detailed internal process, and a connected community of vendors to get the job done. For nearly a decade this had been our work—our trowel.

But before using our trowel as a sword, we had to first identify where the exposed places in our city were—the places where Satan robs, kills, and destroys. We realized that this place was the local abortion clinic. In Isaiah 1:15 we saw that God will not listen to our prayers or pay attention to our solemn assemblies if we turn a blind eye to the shedding of innocent blood. So if we wanted the fruits of 2 Chronicles 7:14 in our city, we needed to do something about the innocent blood of the unborn.

Unfortunately Charlotte consistently leads the state in the total number of abortions. With nearly thirteen hundred churches surrounding three abortion clinics, our city terminated 8,103 babies in 2012 alone.[4] For us, there was no other place in our city where the life-giving power of God's sword needed to go—to breathe life.

 It's one thing to be against murder (abortion), but it's another thing to bring life. That's what Jesus does—He defeats death and He brings life. One of the core business principles we teach is to breathe life. We say "breathe" life because it should come as naturally to us as breathing—that wherever we go, we "breathe" the life of Jesus into our city. This is what being profitable truly looks like.

Proud to be Texans in our backyard in Garland—bet you can't tell which one's which!

With our sister Tracy on Easter Sunday at our house in Kentucky

Getting into shape with our dad—check out his coach shorts!

At the Rangers' stadium as high schoolers with our dad, building our dream of playing in the big leagues

Jason as a freshman at Liberty University, throwing out a runner

David's first Major League Baseball game during spring training with Boston, 1999

Sophomores at Garland Christian Academy, thinking we're so cool!

Our first minor league game against each other

Jason's first year with the Orioles—the Appalachian League in Bluefield, WV

David, at major league spring training with St. Louis, alongside baseball legend Mark McGwire

David and Mike Matheny (St. Louis Cardinals), wrapping up catchers practice

The day before the 2012 Democratic National Convention, leading Charlotte714—the solemn assembly with nine thousand Christians

Being honored by Liberty University at its 2014 commencement, just days after being fired from HGTV

About to go *live!* with Megyn Kelly, Fox News

© JONATHAN VOLK PHOTOGRAPHY

About to do some pull-ups for an HGTV commercial

JESSE VOLK

Filming the show's opening scene with our family around the kitchen island

Day one of filming *Flip It Forward*—we loved our camera crew!

The cover of one of Charlotte's local magazines after our show was announced...

Filming back-scenes family footage for episode #3

Filming for a commercial, highlighting our *competitive* nature

Lots of laughs on set as we made fun of each other during interviews

David and Lori's family: (left to right) Bailey, Ella, Chase, Ava, and Ty

David and Lori—BFF since 1998

Jason and Tori—BFF since 1999

Jason and Tori's family: (left to right) Trae, Jake, Allie, and Lundi

So what was our battle plan to breathe life at this exposed place? We simply took our trowel and made it a sword. By establishing a clear biblical vision, a detailed internal process of ministry, and a community of connected pro-life ministries willing to help abortion-minded mothers in Charlotte, Cities4Life was born. Our trowel had become a sword.

Our vision was simple: to love our neighbor as ourselves. Jesus painted a beautiful picture of this by telling a story of a man who was robbed, beaten, and left for dead in a ditch. Interestingly, a priest and Levite (God's ordained servants) walked by on the other side. The priest might have preached an amazing sermon the next Sabbath on helping our neighbor in the ditch while the Levite followed with a song about the same. But it was the Samaritan who loved his neighbor more. Why? He looked at the man in the ditch and was filled with so much compassion that he went into the ditch, bandaged the man's wounds, took him to an inn, paid for his care, and said he would follow up (Luke 10:27–37). He actually *did* something about the man in the ditch.

When we realized that thousands of our neighbors were being left in the ditches of our city while many of God's people walked by on the other side, we knew this exposed place needed to become our mission field. And when we saw the abortion clinic as a place of mission—not a place of protest—we didn't have to reinvent the wheel to fight this battle. We just replicated the story of the good Samaritan.

The model Cities4Life provides is simple. We connect abortion clinics (ditches)—where moms, unborn babies, and families are being robbed, beaten, and left for dead, so to speak—to the Life Network—a community of pro-life ministries (good Samaritans) dedicated to loving their neighbors. This network includes pro-life doctors, baby shower ministries, adoption services, housing assistance programs, mobile sonogram units, and more. We simply made the theology of the good Samaritan our biography at the exposed place in our city, right at the abortion clinic.

Maybe the images flashing through your head right now are of protesting and marching with picket signs, but that's not the case. At one time the church in America thought this was the right approach. But abortion is not a political issue—it's a gospel issue. Therefore, we can't fight politically through protests and picket signs (though voicing our pro-life position and electing pro-life leaders is vital). We must fight with the gospel, which is to love our neighbor as ourselves and help these women in need, right in the ditch where they are.

In order to achieve this gospel-centered approach, we developed our Cities4Life Code of Conduct, which states how missionaries to the unborn are to conduct themselves in a way worthy of Christ while ministering at the clinic (Appendix C). This code has helped establish a God-honoring presence at a very dark, exposed place.[5]

When an abortion-determined mother arrives at the clinic, she often thinks she has no help, but when she talks to a sidewalk counselor, she realizes just how much help she really has. And she also has a new friend who provides her cell number to the mom and follows up by connecting her to the Life Network. This is a simple way to love our neighbor as ourselves at an exposed place in our city. Although Cities4Life is not perfect, this holistic approach has yielded incredible fruit.

Satan hates it when the church acts like Christ, so he continues to create a false perception in the minds of Christians about ministries at these exposed places. But remember, perception is *not* reality. We realize there are plenty of well-intentioned pro-life people still protesting and demonstrating at clinics—and even some not so well-intentioned—but the reality is that we can show them a better way, a more loving way as Christ outlined for us with the good Samaritan. We can't continue to walk by on the other side of the street anymore and say it's not our calling. Love looks like something, and it doesn't leave exposed places wide open for the enemy to come in and steal, kill, and destroy innocent lives.

WHEN YOU PICK UP YOUR SWORD TO FIGHT IN THE EXPOSED places of your city, it will cost you something. The question is, will you obey whatever the cost? I (David) had to answer this question not long after we started Cities4Life, which came full circle when HGTV decided to fire us.

 How you see the battle determines how you fight it. If you see it as a physical battle only, then you will pick up the wrong weapon, just as Peter did when he cut off the ear of the servant to the high priest (John 18:10). But if you see it as a spiritual one, then you will pick up the right weapon and fight it with the right weapon—truth and love. You can't be in the Spirit and be hateful at the same time.

Later, during the May 2014 media firestorm concerning HGTV (which we'll tell you more about later), I was mischaracterized as protesting in front of an abortion clinic. The following is what really happened.

Similar to the horrific Kermit Gosnell "house of horrors" abortion clinic in Philadelphia, the Charlotte clinic where we were ministering was hurting women and disposing of aborted babies in horrendous ways. The North Carolina Department of Health was alerted to the conditions of this clinic and temporarily shut it down. For a day and a half, this exposed place was not exposed anymore. It was a brief but satisfying moment for all of us.

During the shutdown, my dad held a press conference outside on the sidewalk in front of the clinic. He asked me to speak, and I simply outlined what the clinic did and how it was hurting women. I also spoke about why we should be involved in ministry there and how we were to do it in a loving way.

Someone videotaped my sidewalk speech and posted it on YouTube. After watching it, I felt that what I said was accurate and loving, so I decided to keep it online. But deep inside I didn't want people seeing me in front of an abortion clinic standing and speaking as if I was some old-school protestor. (I could feel a Peter-denies-Christ moment coming on.) I was comfortable being a recognized Christian business leader, and I didn't want to "lower" my image by being at an abortion clinic. Being a protestor wasn't my heart, and I also knew the perception of me could be distorted or misinterpreted. I struggled with this for several months.

One more thing happened in that season of time following Charlotte714. Three months after the solemn assembly, we got a phone call from a television production company—something about us doing a reality TV show. We figured there had to be a catch!

FIFTEEN

REAL ESTATE REALI-TV

A New Chapter Begins

But seek first His kingdom and His righteousness,
and all these things will be added to you.
—Matthew 6:33

 When we focus on God's stuff, He will handle our stuff.
#LetGodBringItToYou

WHO WOULD HAVE THOUGHT THAT A NEW DREAM COULD EMERGE for us, one even bigger than the major leagues? Just three months after Charlotte714 and in the middle of building Cities4Life, we got a phone call from a production company. The folks on the other end of the call said they had read articles about our successful real estate work and enjoyed watching some of the videos on our website.

"We'd like to interview you guys," they said. "Would you be interested in doing reality television?"

For a moment we saw flashes of greatness streak through our minds and feelings of deep satisfaction that we could potentially become reality stars. I mean, come on—how would you have felt if someone asked you if you were interested in a reality show? (David: It was finally the big break Jason had been waiting for! Ha!)

Our internal answer was, *Heck yes, we're interested . . . and it's about time you called!* But we simply responded with a polite, "No, thanks." We just knew there was a catch. It was too good to be true, and "hope deferred makes the heart sick" (Proverbs 13:12). So we knew better than to get our hopes up.

Yet this production company was persistent and called us back. They assured us there was no catch, so we decided to do an interview. After an hour on Skype they wanted more time with us—next time with our wives. We knew that once they saw our wives and talked with them it was a done deal—and sure enough, we were right.

They loved the idea of twins who were in business together, highly competitive, happily married with nine combined children, and who lived on the same street. They pitched the idea of a show with our family to the president of their company, and he gave them the green light to produce a "sizzle."

The only thing we knew about *sizzle* was waking up on Saturday morning with our mom frying bacon in a pan—and saving the grease to put on our eggs. But in the television industry, a sizzle clip is a short teaser video pitched to networks that highlights potential talent and elements of a would-be show. So the production company produced a sizzle clip on us and took it to a pitch fest in LA where all the networks were gathered to find the next *Duck Dynasty*. And then . . . *boom!* Within a few days they called to say, "Five networks are really interested, and with the positive reviews we're receiving, we might want to think about a talent agent." *Excited* doesn't quite describe what we were after hearing that. (Jason: It was only a three-minute clip, so they didn't have an opportunity to realize David has a snaggletooth.)

Now keep in mind, a production company is not the same thing as a network. To make a reality TV show, three things are needed: the talent, the production company, and the network. The production company sticks with the talent no matter which network ends up buying the program. They may invest some money in order to get the talent sold to a network, but a show only gets produced once the major funding from a network begins to pour in—and that only happens if a network buys in to the concept of the show and the abilities of the talent. And for that to happen, a lot of market research and due diligence take place within the network. (Sorry, that was a lot of information! But this is how it works in reality showbiz.)

Reality TV programs have been around for nearly two decades, but recent years have brought out at least two shows that revolve around fun and quirky Christian families: the Duggars (*19 Kids & Counting* on TLC) and the Robertsons (*Duck Dynasty* on A&E). There is a strong market for family-centered and faith-based reality TV programming. Anything that isn't moral garbage and portrays real families doing life together—such shows have strong possibilities in terms of market share and popularity. So our production company felt they had a winner with our show.

Within three months after our first phone call with the production team, we received an offer from The Learning Channel (TLC). We're friends with the Duggar family and knew they were pleased with TLC's approach to doing their show, so it looked like we'd be heading there too.

Then at the end of March 2013, as our families were together for one of our kids' birthdays (with nine kids between the two of us, we're always gathering for birthdays), we got a call.

I (David) saw that it was a call from out of town and didn't answer. But the transcript of the message said "HGTV," so I stepped outside to listen. It was one of the managers at HGTV. She said she was on vacation and heard that we were about to sign a contract with another network, so she ran back to her hotel to call us. She said, "Please don't sign with anyone until you see an offer from us."

I called her right back. This was my first conversation with an HGTV executive, and everything went great. She said, "Watching your sizzle clip, we see you have such positive energy and lovely families. When you compete with each other, you're using your competition to build each other up, not tear each other down. And do you really live on the same street? You all seem to get along so well." Obviously the sizzle clip didn't highlight the moments when I dominated Jason on the basketball court.

What really excited her was to know that we were real estate professionals with experience in all things real estate. In other words, we weren't actors with smiling faces but empty tool belts. We had real-life expertise HGTV could use to make just about any house-related type of show.

I loved hearing her excitement for our families and business, but I also needed to let her know something up front. "My brother and I are men of faith," I told her. "We're not going to browbeat anybody, but we are vocal about our faith. What has led us to our success is applying biblical principles in our business and families. I hope that makes sense."

She said she understood, and we said good-bye.

A few days later our production team called and said, "You're never going to believe it, but you boys just got a crazy offer from HGTV. They're offering to take you straight to series and are offering six one-hour episodes right out of the gate. We don't ever see offers like this!"

Okay, so being newbies, we needed a little more explanation. What does all that mean?

"No pilot," they said. "They're not buying a pilot episode—you're going straight to television. That's how confident they are in this. They want you . . . now."

So at this point in the story we were feeling pretty good. We had offers from TLC and HGTV and were on the verge of a bidding war. Not only could this reality show truly become a reality, but we now had the possibility of being catapulted to the front among all the talent on a major network in pretty short order. It felt like this was even bigger than making it to the major leagues. A new dream for us was born that day.

The next few months were surreal. We had conference calls with executives from both networks, each pitching their network to us. For a while we debated whether TLC might be a better fit for us. But as negotiations continued, we started leaning toward HGTV. They had made us a better offer, and we felt a kindred connection to their team as they continued to reach out and connect with us. At this point we hadn't even determined yet what the show would be—we just knew it would have something to do with real estate. HGTV seemed like a pretty good fit.

While all this was taking place, the business affairs department at HGTV did a background check on us. The Right Wing Watch article resurfaced—the September 6, 2012 article discussed in chapter 14. If you remember, this article featured bits of our initial interview with Janet Mefferd—coming days after Charlotte714 and the Democratic National Convention. The business affairs department sent the article to the HGTV executive team. But that didn't end anything because their response was to simply call and talk with us and see what the article was truly all about.

Before they talked directly with us, they spoke with our production company, which is standard protocol. The show developer at our production company then called us and asked one simple question: "Are you anti-gay?" It took me (Jason) by surprise so much that I was speechless for a second. I responded by saying that we were anti-nothing. We're pro-family guys who believe in the Bible, and we believe marriage is between a man and a woman.

They said, "Well, there's this article on the Internet. HGTV just wants to make sure you guys explain yourselves to them and don't have an agenda against anyone in the gay community." We said, "We've sold over twenty thousand properties nationwide and are respected in our community. You can't do that if you are against people. Our position remains a loving position that God defines both sexuality and family, yet we are *not* anti-gay, nor do we speak against homosexuals as people."

David was in the Philippines at the time, visiting our office there, so I (Jason) shot over a message to him that afternoon: *Call me, dude. HG thinks we're anti-gay.* He called me immediately, and we talked about the possibility of losing a huge platform that we had felt God was giving us and how difficult it would be to let it go.

After that conversation we didn't hear anything more from HGTV for several weeks—or even our production company for that matter. Everything went silent. We felt as though it went from 100 mph to 0 mph in a blink. We figured it was over and we were already pitched to the curb. Once again we found ourselves having to die to yet another dream, one that we had thought would be bigger than them all.

Let's pause for a moment and soak in all that was going on in our heads during this time. We were both so exhilarated about this new platform that we had gotten dizzy with the idea of it. Endless possibilities for ministry, greater impact for God, increased revenue for business—you name it, we were dreaming about it. So this phone call from our production company felt like open-heart surgery without anesthesia. We were deflated. Our commitment to serving Jesus whatever the cost was being put to the test again.

This was a "Peter moment" for us—we felt like denying the Lord or, at least, following Him at a distance.

Out of fear that we could be misunderstood any further, I (David) called our web developer and asked him to take down the Charlotte714 website. I also called a few ministry friends who had blogs or videos of mine and asked them to take them down for a time. I wasn't running away because I thought I was wrong in what I said. I was running away because I was afraid. I considered removing the video of me speaking in front of the abortion clinic, but I hadn't posted it so I didn't have the ability to remove it. And God ended up using it in a big way—despite my cowardice masked as strategic bridge building. See how cowardly we were when we got our eyes off the Person and onto the platform?

We thought about trying to create a positive perception in the media, which is a noble but futile endeavor for Christians. We wanted to recapture this new platform that seemed to have been given to us for a moment and now seemed to be gone. But this approach just didn't fit—it wasn't us, and our dad reminded us of that.

"You boys don't need to be afraid of who you are and whose you are!" Dad told us. "God has made you bold for a reason and for a season—and now is the time you need to stand up and be the men God made you to be. Our nation needs strong leaders, the church needs courage, and you need to be men of God who run to the roar!" We knew that our dad was speaking the truth, but we felt that a softer, more attractive approach could possibly be a better strategy. It was as if we were trying to braid the mane of the Lion of the Tribe of Judah! (This title is used in Revelation 5:5, in reference to Jesus.)

It's natural to let the *purpose* of God replace the *Person* of God. This only happens when our focus is on the purpose of God and not the God of purpose. When we do this, we begin transacting with God at the level of the mind and no longer at the level of the heart. Things then have to make sense for us before we follow God, and strategy overtakes the Spirit. But when our focus remains on the Person of God and we let His purposes follow in the wake, then we will transact with Him at the level of the heart. We'll obey Him whatever the cost even if it doesn't make sense in our minds. We seek to live Person-driven lives—we let the Person of God take control of His purposes for us.

Back to the story. We both knew that it was simply a matter of time before the agenda to silence our beliefs would find us and try to shut us up. The question was, would we be willing to face it? Were we truly willing to face our fears and follow Jesus whatever the cost?

I (Jason) wrote in my journal on April 18, 2013:

It's just crazy how much emotional stress this has caused us. I said to Tori that it feels just like a breakup! Like, my heart feels ripped apart in the same way it would feel if she were to break up with me when we were dating. I know it's just an emotion and that it will pass with time, but during this time it has been much harder than we imagined. We still haven't heard back from either network or our production company. Nobody is talking with us and we're getting crazy mixed signals. The feeling we have is that they have all abandoned us in fear. It's been a really tough road, but one that I definitely believe God has orchestrated. The great part about this is that David and I are discovering so much about ourselves, and God is teaching us some very valuable lessons.

Twelve things we learned during this time:

1. When a vision is birthed and we die to it, if it resurrects itself, we need to stay dead to it in our hearts.
2. Don't let a thirst for influence turn into a lust for influence. We need to go after the God of influence and not the influence that God gives.
3. Ambition is a great follower but a terrible leader. We need to die to selfish ambition.
4. We need to keep focusing on depth and let God handle our breadth.
5. We need to be faithful to keep doing what we've always done and not move on to the next thing (pick the broomstick back up and be faithful in little things).
6. When *want* enters the picture—we want things we didn't used to want—remember this: "The LORD is my shepherd, / I shall *not* want" (Psalm 23:1).
7. Being wanted feels good, but it can lead to being a people-pleaser.
8. Being a "living" sacrifice (Romans 12:1) is all about faithfulness because when the heat turns up, we want to hop off the altar.
9. Reframe! We need to reframe difficult situations in our minds—is it really so bad? Not in light of all the pain Christ went through for us.
10. Be careful not to fear man more than God—being worried about what people think instead of what God thinks.
11. We must decrease, and He must increase. Avoid the temptation to think we must increase so He can increase. That's dumb!

12. Emotions take time—healing often happens long before you *feel* healed.

It took several weeks for us to get through the death of this new dream and stand back on our own two feet again. We were both down, and while we were down, we made some dumb, cowardly decisions—like shutting down the Charlotte714 website. But God is faithful, and He loves His children too much to let them run away from who they are in Him!

It was time for us to die to another dream, face our fears, and live powerfully for Him. Although it took a few weeks, that is exactly what we chose to do.

 Boldness apart from brokenness makes a bully. God must first break us so that He can use us. He did the same with Peter, and on the foundation of Peter's brokenness God used him to help build the church, even though he denied Him three times. A broken man is a powerful man, one who can be as bold as a lion.

Having gone through a brief Peter moment of denial and brokenness, we began to feel a supernatural boldness coming back to us. We felt God say to us that He was the one who gives platforms and takes them away—all in His timing and according to His ways. We aren't to change who we are. We're to be the men of God He made us to be, strong in the face of evil and willing to lay our lives down for others.

Standing on this platform of courage, we were prepared for what was coming next.

OUT OF THE BLUE, HGTV E-MAILED US AND ASKED IF WE COULD meet in person with them in Nashville. After weeks of silence we thought the show was dead, so we didn't know what the meeting was all about. We had business clients in Nashville anyway, so a quick trip there worked out perfectly for us.

We rolled up to the restaurant and met with the man who would become the executive producer of our show. And right out of the gate he said, "Guys, are you choosing us or not? We thought maybe you guys weren't interested in us and had chosen another network after all."

Are you serious? Hold up! Roller coasters are scary, but this roller coaster was taking us for a wild ride. The shot of adrenaline that surged through our bodies could've lit up a small city. We were back in the game. The only words that could describe it are the best two words in our vocabulary: *Booya Grandma!*

We told him that HGTV's perception of our interest wasn't the case at all and that we had been waiting for them to contact us. We then reiterated to him what we had told the production company about our beliefs. We wanted to make sure there was no stone left unturned about where our beliefs collided with the hot-button issues of our day.

He said, "You guys sure don't come across as anti-anything. We've gotten to know you a bit and would like to have you as part of our network. We just want to make sure you don't have an agenda."

We looked him dead in the eye and explained, "We love people because Jesus loves people. But Jesus does not love all ideas, nor do we."

"As long as you guys have no agenda," he said, "then you're not going to be saying things on the show about how you don't believe in homosexuality."

Of course we weren't going to do that because we don't do that in real life. This is a reality show, right? We didn't sell thousands of houses by telling everyone what we believe about sexuality.

When the meeting ended that day, we called our agents and our production company and told them we were definitely going with HGTV, yet they still had TLC on the line. After calling and delivering the news to TLC, our agents gave us the green light to call our show executive at HGTV with our verbal acceptance.

Here's an interesting point: the contract came to us in June, yet we didn't get it signed until December. There's a lot of back-and-forth involved in the process of hammering out who is doing what: network, production company, and talent. These things take time. The process isn't an impulse, like deciding to buy a pack of gum at the checkout lane. Both parties to the contract—HGTV and the Benhams—took their time in thinking this through.

During the months between the initial contract (June) and the final contract (December), we tweeted and blogged away business as usual. We were still tweeting Bible verses and blogging biblical principles. Nothing changed. Nothing was different. Now the HGTV folks and our production company were following us on these social media platforms. But there was no outcry or accusation of our being too Christian or too radical.

To give you some idea of the kind of financial commitment being made here, we've been told that reality TV shows range anywhere from $250,000 to $400,000 per episode to produce, depending on how much marketing goes into the show. Calculate the funds needed for six one-hour episodes, and you'll have an idea how committed HGTV was to us and how committed we were to them.

All that to say, HGTV supported us and planned on making a show they believed would be entertaining to audiences and profitable for their company. And when we officially signed with them, we were welcomed into their family with open arms.

SIXTEEN

THE BREAKUP

Getting Fired

And they all left him and fled.
—Mark 14:50

 Brave people are those who have simply taken dominion over their inner coward. Bravery is a matter of dominion, not strength. #DominionLeadstoBravery

"WHAT DO YOU THINK ABOUT ALL THE STUFF THAT HAPPENED OVER at A&E?" one of the executives at HGTV asked us over lunch just before we started filming our show. "The big blowup over Phil Robertson's interview in GQ?"

It was the third week in March 2014—just a few weeks before we started filming—and we were eating a meal in Knoxville with the HGTV executive team. You may remember what happened at the end of 2013, when Phil Robertson, the *Duck Dynasty* patriarch, sat down in his home with a GQ reporter. Robertson's comments came to light on December 18 and prompted A&E to immediately suspend him from the show. Interestingly it was the same week we received our final-form contract fully ratified by HGTV, on December 20. So right as we were finishing up an entire year of negotiation and finalizing the contract for our show, the biggest Christian star of reality TV received a suspension because of comments he made supporting the Bible.

A&E reinstated Robertson a week later (December 27) after 250,000 folks signed an "I stand with Phil" online petition. Yet for any Christian considering a future in reality television, that week certainly gave much reason to pause and think about what could happen.

Now three months later, we were at lunch in Knoxville with several HGTV executives. What did they think about the *Duck Dynasty* flap?

"It's just amazing to see where we are in America," one executive said. "Whether you agree with Robertson or not . . . I mean it's just unreal. A&E knew who they were—*everybody* knows who they are—so are there any surprises out there?"

As we wrote in the previous chapter, we had already been asked if we were anti-gay by HGTV, and our response was still the same: "We're not anti-anything—we are pro-Jesus." But at the table that day the conversation was reopened. "Phil has a way with words," we said, "and we certainly agree with his beliefs about the issue." The conversation was filled with grace all the way around the table, and the team at HGTV heard once again about our love for Jesus as well as all people, without compromising on the issue.

It seems that if a Christian has a biblically informed opinion on the topics of marriage and unborn life, then there is reason for them to hesitate voicing their beliefs. These two areas are at the center of incredible controversy today—and if you define these issues the way God defines them, you become a cultural outcast. But those who fear God recognize that this is a spiritual battle, one that must be fought spiritually by those who are "battle ready." And to be battle ready, we must know the cost up front and be willing—for the sake of Jesus Christ—to pay the price whatever the cost.

 Iron sharpens iron (Proverbs 27:17); marshmallows don't sharpen marshmallows. For iron to be sharpened it must clash with another piece of iron—this is healthy.

Spiritual and intellectual progress stops the minute you silence one side of the debate. We all need to toughen up a bit and let our ideas clash for the health of the church and the nation.

AFTER LUNCH WITH OUR EXECS WE WENT BACK TO CHARLOTTE IN hopes of becoming big-time reality TV stars, or so we thought. The dream only lasted a few months—so don't blink, or you'll miss it. One interesting fact is that we didn't have a show concept until a few months before we started filming. And even that one changed a few weeks before our first day on set. HGTV eventually landed on the concept of the two of us teaching families how to flip houses, hence the name *Flip It Forward*. Episodes were to be jam-packed with white-knuckled demolition, heart-pounding CrossFit workouts, pristine renovations, and tons of family fun and sibling rivalry. We couldn't wait to start filming!

We finished all the preproduction work by the middle of March 2014 and began filming the first week of April. Six house-flipping families were ready to go with their properties, and everyone was stoked! Of course, the world didn't yet know about the show. Publicity rollout of a show doesn't happen until after the filming starts.

By the way, if you pay attention to cultural flash points in the news, the first week of April 2014—our first week of filming—was significant. That was the same week that Brendan Eich, cofounder and CEO of software company Mozilla, was forced out of his position with the company after it was discovered he had supported the 2008 California Proposition 8—defining marriage as between a man and a woman. The cultural polarization on these issues kept intensifying with the passing of each month.

Meanwhile, we were standing in front of production lights and cameras all day long—doing our shtick to create the first six episodes of the show. We were rookies, but we were soaking it all in.

I (Jason) wrote in my journal on April 16, 2014:

We're almost two full weeks into shooting. It has been a crazy experience. There are cameras all over us—we are "the talent"! Ha! Funny to be called that. We've learned a lot and have slowly gotten more comfortable being on camera—you basically have to get to where you don't even know they are filming you. For me, it has gotten easier the more I don't care what others think. In the first few days of shooting, I was pretty self-conscious: "What does my face look like? Do I need to lose weight? I don't want to say anything stupid. Dude, Tom Cruise probably loves HG and will be watching us, so I want to do a good job . . ." Thoughts like this made me clam up. I realized that the more self-conscious I was the less creative I was, and God made David and me creative and fun when we're around people. But as I threw off self-consciousness and started focusing more on honoring God I got looser. It's been great! I've been focusing on the fact that this new season of life was brought to us by God, and that it's for a specific reason. All David and I have to do is be ourselves. We don't have to change for the camera. If people don't like us, then *so what!*

As we were having a blast through long days of filming, our show executive from HGTV flew in from Knoxville. He said he wanted to take us to dinner after we wrapped up production for the day. So he was on the set all day as we were doing our dead-level best not to mess this thing up! Mind you, we were rookies at being on camera, and until you've had cameras shoved in your face for a long period of time, you have no clue how self-conscious you can get, especially when the exec who hired you is watching your every move in the film truck outside.

A quick behind-the-scenes story—we did a lot of crazy stuff on camera. On this particular day while our exec was in town, we decided to do a "toes to bar" competition where we jump and grab a pull-up bar—in this case a rafter in the carport—to see who could touch his toes to it the most times. It was silly, but it was a great way to let out some of our competitive nature. Well, I (Jason) can knock those out in my sleep, but for some reason I started swaying badly, and then all of a sudden—*boom!* I dropped eight feet and landed flat on my back. The funny part was that our director held back everyone from helping me until the camera guys captured the shot! Now that's the price you pay for good TV. Whatever the cost, right?

Back to the story. We wrapped for the day and headed out to dinner with our exec. Just as we were about to dive in to our steaks, he told us the show was going to the upfronts in New York: "Nobody knows you right now, but very soon millions of people are going to discover you." Upfronts are publicity events that give networks the chance to highlight future shows to secure advertising dollars, from Chicago and Dallas to Boston and LA.

Then his tone turned a bit more serious: "We've been following your Twitter posts. . . . We don't mind you talking about your faith, but speaking about the controversial stuff may give people the impression that you're 'haters.'" Our hearts started to beat pretty fast at this point. We thought, *Oh boy, here we go again. It's coming.*

You have to remember, he is our network executive—and by now, our friend. He's the one HGTV was looking to for the production of our show. We loved him and were immediately concerned about how our convictions might end up putting his own job on the line. It's one thing to be willing to pay the price when it's your own skin, but when there comes potential for collateral damage to others as well, the stakes become higher.

 The secret to experiencing the power of God in your life is through total surrender. This means giving everything we have to God, whatever the cost. Sometimes our decision to surrender to Jesus may cost others, too, which is precisely why many of us hold back. We may not mind paying the price of total surrender ourselves, but it's very difficult when others have to pay it as well.

When our executive made this comment, several Bible stories came rushing to our minds. We were reminded of Esther, who, after becoming the queen of Persia, did not reveal her Jewish ancestry to the king. When a plot to destroy the Jews surfaced, Esther's cousin Mordecai sent word to her of the plan and told her she needed to plead with the king for the life of her people. She pointed out to Mordecai that she could be killed for doing that. This was Esther's first response. She didn't want to face her fear of being killed. We can understand that.

That's when Mordecai reminded her of the connection between our faithful obedience to God and His own actions in the world. He simply reminded her of who she was by saying, "Do not imagine that you in the king's palace can escape any more than all the Jews. For if you remain silent at this time, relief and deliverance will arise for the Jews from another place and you and your father's house will perish. And who knows whether you have not attained royalty for such a time as this?" (Esther 4:13–14).

Boosted in her spirit by the courageous convictions of Mordecai, Esther's second response to him came loaded with the courage of a battle-ready warrior. She said, "I will go in to the king, which is not according to the law; and if I perish, I perish" (Esther 4:16). She decided to face her fears.

Sitting at the table in uptown Charlotte that night, we experienced our own "Esther moment" of contemplating how to save our own skin. Then we remembered that we were born for a time such as this, so we decided to face our fears of losing the show.

As we were sitting there, we felt as though we were at the same spot eight months earlier when our production company had asked us, "Are you anti-gay?" All the feelings we had during those weeks we thought we had lost the show came rushing back—except now they were compressed into the span of a few seconds. The fear of losing something you desire is a strong emotion. Yet we both dug in our heels and prepared to stand our ground.

We felt a supernatural courage rising up within us, and it came because we already had committed ourselves in our minds to a "whatever the cost, we're following Jesus" way of living. One minute we were waffling, but the next minute we felt like we had galvanized courage in our backbones—courage that could not be broken.

Remember in the movie *Wolverine*, where Hugh Jackman's character is put in a tank full of water so that his bones could be converted into adamantium metal? (*Wow!*—that's a big word for guys like us.) What a rocking part of the movie! While he was in the tank, his bones were converted into an indestructible liquid metal that turned him into a wrecking ball. That's what we felt happen in that moment sitting in the restaurant. All feelings of fear were now gone, and we were ready to live powerfully for Jesus. We remembered who we were—followers of Christ—and that made all the difference. Powerful resolve comes on the other side of remembering our true identity.

Having been poked about our beliefs at least three times now, we realized this wasn't going away. Winsome and graceful communication is always the proper course of action for a Christian, but it only has power when coupled with honesty, forthrightness, and integrity of conviction. I (David) will never forget that dinner. It prepared us for what was coming. People say, "Wow, it must have been awful when you got fired by HGTV." Not really. The dinner with our executive several weeks before was much more difficult, when our commitment to follow Jesus whatever the cost was put to the test.

Do you remember when we talked about having a Peter moment in the previous chapter? Well, it presented itself to us again, as it does throughout the life of every believer. We can't stress strongly enough that if God is going to use you, you will go through Peter moments—whether public or private—where you are tempted to deny the Lord. But we cannot forget that Peter was also Christ's most courageous follower. So if you've denied the Lord as Peter did and then repented, you can also experience the supernatural boldness to stand for the Lord as Peter later did too. Having followed Peter's example in his denials, we were now ready to follow Peter's example in his boldness. (Jason: Throughout my baseball career I had Mark 14:50, "And they all left him and fled," written on my glove as a reminder of the Christ-denier I could be at a moment's notice. This is a verse that reminds me of the kind of guy I am, except for Christ in me.)

At this point in the dinner we asked our show exec an important question: "What would happen if a reporter asked us our thoughts on some of the controversial issues, and we simply opened our Bible and read it without saying anything else—could we do that? What if we read 1 Corinthians 6:9–11 and said nothing else? Can we even do that?" That was the question we put on the table. We then quoted the passage.

As he was sitting there, he leaned back and sighed with a sense of quiet resignation and lack of hope. "Guys, that's a tough one," he said. We knew right then and there that it was all over.

I (Jason) leaned over and said to the executive, "They're going to come after you. They won't come after us first—they're going to go after HGTV. They're going to lump you in with us because you gave us a platform."

In my journal that night I wrote:

It feels as though David and I will soon be entering enemy territory. I'm sure the fight is coming. HGTV has already spoken with us three times about our "rhetoric." One of the higher-ups didn't like that we called abortion a holocaust. And so it begins!

SEVENTEEN

DYING AGAIN

When the Heat Turned Up

The Lord *gave and the* Lord *has taken away.*
Blessed *be the name of the* Lord.

—Job 1:21

When the heat turns up, living sacrifices always want
to crawl off the altar. #DontCrawlOff

WHEN OUR EXECUTIVE PRODUCER SAID WE WERE ABOUT TO BE known by millions of people, he was talking about not only the October premiere of the show but also the upfronts that are held every year in several cities. HGTV hosts theirs through March and early April and chose to introduce our show in New York City, April 23, 2014, two weeks after the dinner conversation from the previous chapter.

The initial response from advertisers was positive, but not everyone was excited. A group called GLAAD (Gay and Lesbian Alliance Against Defamation) immediately went into action lobbying HGTV behind the scenes to have the show pulled. They felt they needed to expose the so-called *hateful* views of the Benham brothers to the executives at HGTV.

But what they failed to realize was that by this time HGTV had already spent over a year with us and knew exactly who we were. For them, *Flip It Forward* was a winner.

A week after the upfronts in NYC, we were in the middle of a day's worth of filming when we got a call from our executive producer. We knew something was wrong. He said GLAAD was extremely upset and demanded a response.

We weren't surprised and simply reminded him we knew this was coming at some point. GLAAD really wanted us out, and HGTV needed to give them a response about our show.

Once GLAAD began putting pressure on HGTV, we realized the battle was coming to us. No amount of verbal temperance could move us into a position of being acceptable to GLAAD. The problem wasn't that we *had* an opinion—the problem was that we *voiced* our opinion. And that wasn't going to stop, especially because what we were speaking is truth that sets people free.

BEFORE WE MOVE ANY FURTHER, I (DAVID) WANT TO TELL YOU AN important piece of this story that should let you see how a person's courage of conviction ebbs and flows. To accomplish this, allow me to share something really personal with you. After our dinner meeting I drafted an e-mail that I never sent. Or at least I never sent it to the HGTV executive as I had planned.

I began to think that maybe we really weren't being asked to compromise the gospel. Maybe our tone just needed to be tweaked. Maybe our response to this situation should be to repackage the message of truth. I mean, my family knows my mouth can get me into trouble in ways that aren't God-honoring. (Jason: I could write a book on the subject.)

I felt like maybe some of my tweets could be misinterpreted, so I deleted a couple of them so my show executive wouldn't lose any more sleep. Then I drafted an e-mail to our executives addressing the negative perception GLAAD was giving them—but I never sent it.

After I drafted the e-mail, I was uncomfortable in my spirit about it. What I wrote was correct, but my motive was wrong—I wanted to manage how I was perceived, and I was doing it out of the fear of man and not in the fear of God. My motive behind the e-mail was self-preservation, which is wrong if you've decided to live for Jesus whatever the cost. I realized that fear is a matter of focus—the more I focused on the show, the more I was afraid to lose it.

I shot the e-mail to a good friend of ours, a spiritual leader over us for about a decade. I asked for his opinion of my e-mail. He replied within two hours, and I was not surprised by his response. His final paragraph summed it up:

> This actually sounds like the type of thing you would shake your head at and associate with some seeker-sensitive church somewhere. And it also means you're compromising your convictions for the sake of TV exposure, which will allegedly get you a greater platform for the gospel, which is kind of like adding pornography sales to your business to generate more income to give to the poor.

My friend and Christian mentor knew I was flirting with compromising my beliefs and my very conscience. I had the fear of man and a man-pleasing spirit, which is a powerful emotion that is debilitating both spiritually and emotionally.

The fear of man in me was in a very small dose, but my friend picked up on it and helped me identify it. So I chose not to send the e-mail. Instead, I asked God to forgive me.

We've heard it said, "A friend is someone who knows the song in your heart and can sing it back to you when you've forgotten the words." Thank God for good friends.

Throughout our story you see several times when we've lacked both discernment and courage. To be honest, we have so many of these instances we could write a book just on the stupid things we've said and done. But God has always been faithful to us, in spite of ourselves.

As He did with Peter, God has been faithful to provide us with just enough wisdom and the necessary courage to bring us through to the other side of cowardly capitulation. We simply needed to ask God for an increase in boldness and to always be ready to follow Jesus whatever the cost.

ON THE CALL THE DAY BEFORE GETTING FIRED, OUR SHOW EXECUTIVE asked us, "So would you guys discriminate against having a gay couple on the show?"

Our response was the same one we had given many times before: "First of all, we don't discriminate against anyone. We've sold thousands of houses in less than a decade. We've never given a sexual litmus test to anyone."

"But here's the deal," we continued. "If an outside group is forcing your hand and requiring you to bow to their agenda, no amount of pandering will work in the long run."

We told our executive that this was reality TV, and in reality we sell to all people. However, we said, we would not push anyone's agenda on our show, no matter how much heat we would take for it. After that phone call we began to pray and seek God for wisdom in the situation. I (David) went home and called several friends—well-known leaders with experience being in the spotlight, household names in Christian circles. And all of them said, "Do not bend to the agenda." Every one of them. "Do not bend."

Another HGTV executive called us later that night. We reiterated that we had always sold and would continue to sell houses to every person who comes to us looking for a home. But we made sure to state that as long as we were hosts on HGTV's network, the fight would be coming to their front door.

"So what would you do in reality?" the executive asked us. "Well," we said, "we would gladly sell to a gay person or couple if it was simply in the common course of events, just like we have our entire careers. But if an activist group forced us to do it in order to show the world that we embrace that particular lifestyle, we could not in good conscience agree to that." For us, this was the line.

Because the battle in our culture is a *spiritual* battle (Ephesians 6:12), it is important for marketplace Christians to serve the *physical* needs of everyone, despite their sin. Yet it becomes a spiritual issue when you are asked to support or endorse a lifestyle or idea that is against your conscience by giving them service. This is where the line must be drawn. We've always said that we would sell hamburgers, houses, and hula hoops to anyone, but we would not sell to them if it in some way supported or endorsed ideologies that were against our beliefs.

Our hearts hurt for our show executives. It was a very trying time for them, evidenced by such a late phone call that night in a desperate attempt to keep our show alive. We finished the call by saying, "We're all on the same team here. We will sell a house to whoever is approved for our show, but we will not push an agenda."

The executive thanked us for taking the call. They said their next step would be to go back to GLAAD and continue the conversation about our show. But before hanging up, the executive said, "We want you guys to know that we think you're going to be stars on our network. We're very excited about your show."

Earlier that day one of the members from our production team had reached out to us and said, "Look, this is when it gets real. We knew this would happen as your exposure grew. It may get a little weird, but stay true to who you are. The haters don't know you, and they can't define you. Once the show airs, your actions will define you."

We responded to all this commotion that night by catching some shut-eye. God never sleeps, but it's okay if we do. "In peace I will both lie down and sleep, / For You alone, O LORD, make me to dwell in safety" (Psalm 4:8). The sweetest sleep is done on the pillow of a clean conscience. We slept sweet that night. And good thing because the next five days would be nonstop and life-changing for us.

WHEN WE AWOKE THE NEXT MORNING (MAY 7, 2014), OUR PHONES were blowing up with texts from friends.

Did you see Facebook?

What's up with the show?

What does HGTV mean by their Facebook message?

Talk about another emotional roller coaster. (We're experiencing it all over again as we write this chapter!) Before our heads hit the pillow the previous night, we had heard, "You're going to be stars on our network." As soon as our eyes opened the next day, we saw, *"We are reviewing the Benham Brothers' show"* on HGTV's Facebook page. We could hear the slowly fading "Booya Grandma!" of having our own show drift into the blackness of "See ya, boys!"

We had no idea what happened. The only thing we could figure was that GLAAD must not have been happy with the conversation they'd had with HGTV the previous night.

Around noon that day, as we wrapped filming for lunch, we got a text asking us to hop on a call with three HGTV executives. So we skipped lunch with the crew and drove back to Jason's house to spend time in prayer before the call. After praying, we got off our knees, dialed the number, and turned on the speakerphone . . .

"Guys, I wish we had better news, but we have chosen not to continue with the show." No small talk. No prepping the needle. Just a straight-out breakup! We had never been dumped before, but this was a bad one, and it was in front of the watching world—at least, it was about to be.

We took a deep breath and said, "Thank you. Thank you for giving us this opportunity. Thank you for believing in us. Thank you for taking the chance and investing so much in us. We have no regrets, and we have no ill feelings toward you guys at all. We love you guys, and you will all be a part of our story forever."

We meant every word of that, and we still do. The executives at HGTV were wonderful people. They are the ones who won us over. We'll always have a special place in our hearts for them.

The spokesperson said, "I was not anticipating being speechless on this call." Evidently they were anticipating some fireworks and fury.

The other executive, the one who told us the night before that we were going to be stars, said, "I'm fighting back tears right now. I just can't believe all this is happening."

Another executive, our friend and the one who had worked to coach us during the dinner sessions, wasn't able to say anything at all. Not one word. It hurt. We really felt bad for him because he had put so much time and energy into our show and now realized it was all for nothing. These are real people who invest themselves in their work, so the cancellation of the show was a kick in the gut to everyone involved.

We ended the call with some more expressions of gratitude, but we never really got to the bottom of why the decision had been made. In fact, we didn't even talk about it. We just figured it was from the old Right Wing Watch article written after Charlotte714, though we couldn't really understand how a two-year-old blog post could've been such a fresh powder keg of destruction. After all, nine months earlier we had already talked with HGTV about it, and everything seemed okay.

Our guess was wrong. Right Wing Watch had posted a new article the night before. After this post, a mass of people began blowing up HGTV's Facebook page while we—and most of America—were sleeping. This is the reason HGTV posted, "We are reviewing the Benham Brothers' show" on their Facebook page early the next morning—the morning of our breakup.

Now, by the time we are writing this book, Right Wing Watch has dozens of articles about the Benhams—each one castigating us for holding to basic Christian beliefs that have been held by millions of people for thousands of years.

So it was a new article that had pushed HGTV into the corner, and we knew nothing about it. After we hung up the phone, we called our wives. Tori immediately went on HGTV's Facebook page and followed the links that took her to the Right Wing Watch website. That's where she read the fresh piece: "HGTV Picks Anti-Gay, Anti-Choice Extremist for New Reality TV Show."[1] This new article, written by the same author as the 2012 one, was a train wreck of distortion and smear. The writer used the name "Benham" so loosely that a reader could not tell whether the author was referring to our dad or us—or anyone else. The article made statements none of us has ever said. It was a brilliant piece of propaganda cleverly designed to distort the truth and smear our character. Unfortunately propaganda works in America, and the polarized condition of our nation with animosity toward God's standards is what we have to show for it.

Had HGTV waited long enough to hear from the rest of America, they might have evaluated things differently. But the bullying power of the Right Wing Watch article and the GLAAD network caused HGTV to submit to the demands at the time. It was a well-orchestrated and flawlessly executed hit on Christian values.

We never had a chance to defend ourselves to our HGTV partners. Had we known about the new article when we were on the phone with them earlier that day, we could've set the record straight. But we didn't know about it at that time. We shot an e-mail over to the executives to explain how dishonest the new article was. But we never heard back from them. Once the decision was made, it was final.

That day it seemed every news network in America was calling us to get an interview to hear our side of the story. Although we originally said we didn't want to be involved in a public way for fear of hurting our friends at HGTV, we realized that this story wasn't going away and that HGTV had gotten bullied into this decision. So we posted on our website a simple statement that provided a launching pad for us to set the record straight and stand against this agenda to silence us. Here is that statement, posted at midnight as we headed into Thursday, May 8:

STATEMENT ON HGTV

May 8, 2014

STATEMENT FROM BENHAM BROTHERS:

The first and last thought on our minds as we begin and end each day is, have we shined Christ's light today? Our faith is the fundamental calling in our lives, and the centerpiece of who we are. As Christians we are called to love our fellow man. Anyone who suggests that we hate homosexuals or people of other faiths is either misinformed or lying.

Over the last decade, we've sold thousands of homes with the guiding principle of producing value and breathing life into each family that has crossed our path, and we do not, nor will we ever discriminate against people who do not share our views.

We were saddened to hear HGTV's decision. With all of the grotesque things that can be seen and heard on television today you would think there would be room for two twin brothers who are faithful to our families, committed to biblical principles, and dedicated professionals. If our faith costs us a television show then so be it.

—David & Jason Benham[2]

I (Jason) remember texting David around midnight before I fell asleep. I told him the next morning our lives were going to change forever . . . for the better. We hadn't lost anything—we'd actually gained a whole lot. We were born for a time such as this, and it was an honor to follow Jesus whatever the cost.

EIGHTEEN

RUNNING THROUGH FIRST BASE

Life After Getting Fired

Weeping may last for the night,
But a shout of joy comes in the morning.
—Psalm 30:5

 When you're out before you leave the batter's box, you have a choice to make—do you walk back to the dugout or run through first base? #ChampionsRunThroughFirst

BASEBALL TAUGHT US A LOT ABOUT LIFE. SOME OF THE MOST VALU-able lessons we ever learned were taught on the ball diamond, playing America's favorite pastime. And the most important one is this: always run through first base!

It's incredibly deflating when you hit a sharp ground ball right back to the pitcher—and you know you're out even before you get out of the batter's box. At that moment every baseball player has a choice to make:

run through first or walk back to the dugout. How the hitter responds in this situation tells you a lot about the kind of person he is.

One thing we know that resonates in the hearts of all baseball lovers: losers give up and pout their way back to the dugout, but champions hustle through first base regardless of how deflated they feel. This, according to our coach/dad, was one of the best ways to win over yourself.

Fast-forward twenty-five years after little league. Getting fired by HGTV five weeks into filming without airing the first episode felt eerily similar to the lessons we'd learned as young baseball players. We thank God we learned how to run through first base, which guided our actions to move beyond our emotions. It's difficult when you put your heart and soul into something, only to have it snatched from you before it even begins. The dream of becoming reality TV stars had trumped our dream of becoming Major League Baseball players, yet we had to die to this dream and make the tough decision to run through first base, just days after getting fired.

We had committed to help six families learn how to flip houses, and we weren't about to walk back to the dugout now. So we got our feet moving down the first-base line and gathered the families in our office for a private meeting. Although they seemed disappointed in HGTV's decision, between laughs and tears we all committed to stay together and finish strong. We offered our services for free, agreeing to market the properties for no commission, even though we were not contractually bound to do so.

Christians in the marketplace are to operate according to a covenant and not simply a contract. Contracts are based on mutual shielding (ensuring that you *get* what you deserve), but covenants are based on mutual yielding (ensuring that you *give* what you have).

Because we operate according to a covenant, which transcends any contract, the decision to continue helping these families was easy to make.

To HGTV's and our production company's credit, they also remained faithful to their financial commitments to help these families until the end. Fortuitously we had the opportunity to publicly thank HGTV on *Fox and Friends*, a grateful acknowledgment that came straight from the heart.

Because we had so many people calling us to get our side of the story and to hear about our next steps, we decided to throw together a quick video about running through first base, called "Finishing What We Started."[1] As we outlined our plans to take care of the families, thousands of viewers had the opportunity to see that our joy hadn't been stripped away by difficult circumstances. God had given us a supernatural grace to die to our dream (loss of the reality show) and face our fears (continual assault on our reputation) in the midst of a fiery ordeal for us.

We also used the video to outline our commitment to three guiding principles that kept our joy abounding—Christ, character, and contentment. These principles allowed us to live from the inside out.

There are many cultural pressures to live according to the world's way today, but focusing on what God thinks and not what others think allows you to live from the inside out instead of the outside in. This eternal perspective allows you to live powerfully, even in the face of fears.

Because Christ is the foundation of our lives, we knew and trusted that He was with us, He had a plan for us, and He was for us. Dozens of scriptures confirmed this truth in our lives. We also knew that trials produce perseverance, and perseverance proven character, and proven character hope (Romans 5:3–4). We had been through so many trials in previous chapters of our lives that God had built just enough *character* into us to help make tough decisions when the heat turned up, which was a miracle in and of itself. And we were truly *content* with or without the show. We had learned "the secret of being content in any and every situation" (Philippians 4:12 NIV) and that "godliness with contentment is great gain" (1 Timothy 6:6 NIV).

Instead of feeling as if we had lost everything, through contentment we were able to reframe the situation to realize that we had really gained much more. This emotion—rooted from years of reading the Bible and time with Jesus—was real for us. It wasn't something we had to drum up with self-talk, but it was a supernatural feeling only the Lord Jesus could give us in the midst of this trial.

The trial produced in our lives two very important fruits that line up with Scripture. First, it strengthened our vertical relationship with God, and second, it strengthened our horizontal relationship with others. We were inundated with Facebook messages and personal notes from many—even in the gay community—saying they were listening intently to our message, which was simply the message of the cross (both a vertical and horizontal piece of wood making its shape).

A few days after we had been fired, Tori and I (Jason) were sitting at home in total peace, without time restraints or pressure to get out the door for more filming. As we were talking and listening to our kids run around outside with their cousins, I said, "There's nowhere else I'd rather be." She replied, "Doesn't it feel good?" I agreed. There's no sweeter feeling than being supernaturally content in the midst of a storm. It's kind of like eating a big piece of dark chocolate right after a sixteen-ounce rib eye.

We never disparaged HGTV for its decision. And we don't have any bitterness in our hearts against the network for how things turned out. Instead, we are truly thankful that God used HGTV to give us a platform to speak the truth in love, at a time when our nation needed it the most, and to get us to where we are now. But that leads to another interesting point.

 We all love it when God uses people's strengths to get us where He wants us, but it's much more difficult when He uses their weaknesses to do it. With an eternal perspective we clearly see that God can and will use *anything* and *anyone* to accomplish His purposes in our lives. We shouldn't get upset if He uses someone's weakness to do the job. If we focus on God's strength as opposed to their weakness, then we'll receive the blessing without the burden of resentment.

During the media firestorm, people were looking at us and saying, "Wow, you're standing in the face of this persecution, with bullets coming at you from all directions, yet you're smiling, speaking truth, and not backing down. Where'd you get this from?" The answer was, time with Jesus, in God's Word and on our knees.

By God's grace, in that moment we were able to see clearly that God was using us as His instruments to bring His kingdom rule to a particular situation. As our King, God had something to say about the spiritual and moral condition of our nation, and He chose to use us to say it. All we had to do was be willing to let Him use us.

Psalm 18:39 says, "You have armed me with strength for the battle; / you have subdued my enemies under my feet" (NLT). This is a promise to all those who dare to face their fears and the real enemy of us all—the one who seeks to steal, kill, and destroy (John 10:10). We felt God's strength in the face of this enemy, and we were emboldened to resist him for God's glory and for the good of others. This is what God's kingdom authority is all about.

IN THE FIRST FEW DAYS AFTER THE CANCELLATION OF THE SHOW, many people asked about the possibility of pitching a new show to a different network. At that point we weren't interested in pursuing another show. We felt like King David must have felt when—as a young boy with a direct path to the throne—he heard Goliath's taunts against the people of God. He cast aside all fear, including the fear of losing his personal future as king, and ran straight toward the giant. He didn't take his personal platform or future promises into account; he simply ran to the roar. At this moment in our lives, we heard our own Goliath—the agenda to silence our beliefs—and his taunts drowned out any desire for personal success.

Yet we really wanted the show to happen and to be everything we dreamed it could be. After all, this was going to become a huge platform for ministry. But we were careful not to let it become our baby, which is very dangerous for leaders. The only way we could keep the show from becoming an idol in our lives was to die to it, and stay dead to it, by holding it with an open hand. This way God wouldn't have to pry our fingers off of it if He wanted to take it away. As Aragorn, one of J. R. R. Tolkien's characters in *The Two Towers*, said, "One who cannot cast away a treasure at need is in fetters."[2]

 God is not going to give you what's in His hand until you let go of what's in yours. The issue isn't, what's in God's hand? The issue is, do you trust God enough to let go of what's in yours?

A great example of holding something with an open hand is found in 2 Samuel 15, where King David's son Absalom had risen up against him and caused David to leave Jerusalem. Behind him followed Zadok the priest and the Levites carrying the ark of the covenant. Verse 25 says, "The king said to Zadok, 'Return the ark of God to the city. If I find favor in the sight of the LORD, then He will bring me back again and show me both it and His habitation.'" David treated the most valuable and powerful earthly possession with an open hand. If he could do that with the ark of the covenant, then we could definitely hold our reality show with an open hand.

As we've said before, the fear of losing what you have, especially if you realize how powerful it could be for God's glory and the good of others, is an incredibly strong emotion. Identifying this fear and facing it head-on is the key to breakthrough. What's on the other side is incredible freedom to be exactly who God created you to be.

Freedom is not the ability to *get* what you *want*, but it's the ability to *give* what you *have*. When you do that, you are truly free.

For most of us, our problem is not as much the fear of losing what we have as it is the fear of man—the desire to please people and to look good in their eyes. Through the process of losing the show, we realized that the "fear of man brings a snare, / But he who trusts in the LORD will be exalted" (Proverbs 29:25). Man-centered fear was a struggle for us to identify and face.

When the platform of a reality show was given to us, we were often willing to sit silent when it came to God's standards in our nation. It was no coincidence that so much cultural debate about God's standards was taking place in our nation at the exact same time we were being handed a platform of national significance. What would we say? Where would we stand?

The only reason we didn't want to speak up was because we were afraid of what others would think or say about us and cause us to lose our show. It was that simple. We had to identify this fear, face it, and choose to fear God and not man. This was and continues to be a battle for us, as it probably is for you as well. But holding what God gives us with an open hand truly helps us become free of this debilitating fear.

Here's what's interesting. After the initial shock of getting dumped wore off, we felt strangely relieved. The umbrella of market-driven coercion was gone. Did we really want to be in a position where we always had to nuance our speaking so as not to offend anyone? Where is the power of the gospel in a nuanced, politically correct approach?

Just when we thought the firestorm was dying down, we got another phone call. One of our longest-standing business clients—having seen the new narrative of the Benham brothers as "haters"—fired us from servicing their foreclosed properties. We were speechless when we were told that all of our properties, along with any properties held by our franchisees, were going to be pulled from us, effective immediately. The reason: "We can hire and fire anyone we choose." However, when the conversation went public, Americans spoke up. In less than twenty-four hours we received a personal apology from the president of the company and all of our properties back. It was amazing to watch.

OVER THE COURSE OF TWO WEEKS AFTER WE WERE FIRED BY HGTV, our media wrap report showed that more than fifty-one million tweets were delivered to Twitter streams relating to our story. America was talking, and people wanted answers. As ABC's *Nightline* put it, "A country founded on freedom of religion and freedom of speech faced fundamental questions."[3]

NINETEEN

BATTLE READY

Whatever the Cost (Until Death)

> Blessed be the LORD, my rock,
> Who trains my hands for war,
> And my fingers for battle.
> —PSALM 144:1

 If you want to dance like David danced, you need to fight like David fought. Don't get your groove on until you get your gear on. #BeAFighter

THE ULTIMATE MOTIVATION FOR ALL CHRISTIANS IS LOVE—LOVE FOR God and for others. But love is not just a feeling or an emotion. Love actually *looks* like something. Jesus gave us a picture of what it looks like when He said, "Greater love has no one than this, that one lay down his life for his friends" (John 15:13). Have you ever stopped to ponder that statement? The ultimate picture of love is to be willing to die for the sake of others. Talk about a sobering reality.

Love doesn't sit back when danger is around, it doesn't cower in the face of fear, and it doesn't look to its own interests above others. No, love looks quite different than that.

On June 6, 1944, the world got a chance to see exactly what love looked like on a day famously known as D-day. The battle of Omaha Beach took place during the Allied invasion of France in World War II. Omaha Beach was six miles wide with huge cliffs overlooking the ocean, which basically made an attack a suicide mission. The Americans had been given the great task of taking this beach. The Germans used dragon's teeth along the shore and heavily armed resistance nests atop the cliffs to build what was one of the most powerfully fortified positions in war history. As our troops hit the beach that day, the German firepower was tremendous. Because gusting winds and strong currents shifted many of our units off course, the troops who hit the beach had little to no cover. At that point they had to make a choice: save their own lives and run for cover, or lay down their lives and "run toward the bullets." I thank God they chose to run toward the bullets. This is what love looked like in 1944: running toward the bullets.

Running toward the bullets is never easy, but it is natural if we are motivated by love. With love our natural reaction to danger is to protect others, not to preserve ourselves. If we are camping with our kids, love would not allow us to sit back if a wolf showed up around the campfire. Love would not compel us to negotiate or find common ground with a rattlesnake if it showed up in our tent. No, love would motivate us to action—to be willing to stand up and step into harm's way for the sake of those we love. Just as it did with our troops on D-day, love calls us to run toward the "bullets" today. And love is willing to fight because love is willing to die.

The picture of love we are seeing from the American church today appears to be quite different than the love Jesus spoke about in John 15:13. We as Christians aren't springing to our feet to stand in the gap against evil. We're not laying down our lives to *be* a blessing—we're often protecting ourselves to *get* the blessing. We have replaced the fear of God with the fear of man—the very thing we have struggled with ourselves. And this man-pleasing spirit has caused an inward focus in many Christians who seek to save only themselves. *We* has been replaced by *Me* in the church today. It's time for a change.

As you've seen throughout this book, dying to yourself is key to living a powerful life. Most of us have never faced the threat of physical death when standing up for what we believe. The cost to us is usually to die to dreams that might've taken first place in our lives, our reputations, or what others thought of us. This pales in comparison to what the faithful witnesses described in Hebrews 11 had to face: "who by faith . . . were tortured . . . experienced mockings and scourgings, yes, also chains and imprisonment. They were stoned, they were sawn in two, they were tempted, they were put to death with the sword. . . . And all these, having gained approval through their faith, did not receive what was promised, because God had provided something better for us" (vv. 33–40).

What a legacy we have! Every one of these people was not only willing to die to his or her dreams and reputations but was also willing to physically die for Christ. These believers were willing to follow Jesus whatever the cost.

Our fight is not against flesh and blood (people) but against demonic forces of darkness (spirits) (Ephesians 6:12). So we need spiritual eyes to see this battle as it manifests in the natural. We saw this firsthand when various media sources lashed out at us for standing up for marriage and the unborn. But we gained strength to stand and fight from 2 Corinthians 10:4–5: "for the weapons of our warfare are not of the flesh, but divinely powerful for the destruction of fortresses. We are destroying speculations and every lofty thing raised up against the knowledge of God, and we are taking every thought captive to the obedience of Christ."

It's interesting that this passage mentions the "destruction of fortresses." A fortress is built when a territory is conquered. This means the conquering king has taken authority over the territory. Our story with HGTV showed the reality of this truth in a painful way as our biblical values were trampled in the media. So the question for us was, what were we supposed to do about it?

Armed with a fresh understanding of 2 Corinthians 10, we knew exactly what to do—destroy Satan's fortress with the truth of God's Word while loving the people held captive under his authority. Our message was very simple: Jesus loves all people (physical), but He does not love all ideas (spiritual). We went into a spiritual battle as we stood on the truth of God's Word, all the while feeling love and compassion for those who differed from us in their beliefs. This is how love led the way for us. We didn't try to balance truth and love—we simply lifted up the name of Jesus because He is the perfect embodiment of both truth and love. But before we had the courage to speak like this, we had to be willing to die to the dream of being HGTV superstars and face the fear of our names being dragged through the mud (a tough lesson to learn, we might add).

Today the battle lines are very clear. If you stand on the truth of God's Word and are willing to voice it publicly, then you will experience this battle. The world will smear your character and create a false narrative about you—and it won't be pretty. Yet we shouldn't be surprised because the Lord said this would happen: "If the world hates you, you know that it has hated Me before it hated you" (John 15:18), and "Blessed are you when people insult you and persecute you, and falsely say all kinds of evil against you because of Me" (Matthew 5:11).

With a quick glance at today's news, we see that Satan is building fortresses and taking dominion in nearly every area of culture. This age-old battle rages for the hearts and minds of people as well as for positions of authority over nations. It seeks to dominate us individually as well as collectively as a nation. As we mentioned in chapter 1, it happened in heaven first, where Satan fought against Christ and His angels for authority in heaven—he lost and was cast down to earth. God then created man and placed him right where He had thrown Satan, and He gave man authority (dominion) over the earth. Yet when Adam stood passively by, watching his wife eat the forbidden fruit, he gave his God-given authority to Satan.

Thus sin entered into the world and death by sin (Romans 5:12). But at the cross, God's Son, Jesus, took the authority back and sealed Satan's defeat forever. Jesus then handed authority to His church to rule on the earth until He returns. This is why Satan attacks the church—he wants the authority back, but he can't have it. Just as Adam's silence gave Satan dominion then, the church's silence gives a portion of it back to him again. (David: Now, that was a lot to chew!)

We are witnesses of how Satan attacks the church to get us to be quiet. We can see this battle raging on three fronts: personal (individual), corporate (the church), and kingdom (nation). And in each of these battlefields Satan's tactic is to distract, deceive, and divide us away from our responsibility as Christians to live and speak the truth that sets people free.

First is the *personal battle*. These are the individual battles we fight every day—the world, the flesh, and the devil (1 John 2:16). We must slay the dragon within before we slay the dragon without. As referenced earlier, we must take "every thought captive to the obedience of Christ" (2 Corinthians 10:5). We must die to ourselves (flesh) daily so that we may live powerfully for God on the other two battlefields. Yet Satan wants us to fail here. He distracts us with all the stuff of the world (fame, fortune, sex, and the rest). He deceives us that these are worth living for and going after. And he seeks to divide us away from our true identity in Christ, rendering us useless. But we have the power of the Holy Spirit! We just need to tap in. Jesus went into the desert "full" of the Holy Spirit and came out in the "power" of the Holy Spirit (Luke 4:1, 14) by defeating Satan's personal attacks on Him. Jesus combated the lies and temptations of the devil with the truth of God's Word. We can experience this same power on a daily basis as we read the Bible, seek God's face, and remain victorious over temptation.

Second is the *corporate battle*. While the personal battle is against individuals, the corporate battle is against the church—the community of believers who make up the body of Christ. We were not meant to fight alone. The gates of hell will not prevail against the church (Matthew

16:18). This is why Satan hates the church. It is in community with the body of believers that we fight *together* against Satan's attacks. The church is the only fighting body that has the supernatural authority to defeat Satan in the earth. The legislative, executive, and judicial branches of government aren't strong enough. Conservative policies aren't strong enough. Only a mature church standing together with one vision and one mission is strong enough to defeat Satan's attacks.

Yet Satan distracts, deceives, and divides us in this battlefield, rendering us useless. He distracts us with our own plans, platforms, and programs in local churches instead of fighting God's battles in culture as the collective church. He deceives us to believe we are not truly in a battle and that we aren't a fighting bride. And he divides us away from our responsibility as salt and light (Matthew 5:13–16), which causes us to lose Christ's authority at the gates of our nation and remain divided in our own ranks.

If the gates of hell will not prevail against the church, then we need to understand what gates were in Jesus' time. A city's gates were the epicenters of activity and influence—they were a combination of city hall, community center, marketplace, and more. We still have city gates today, but they're not entry points into our cities; they are spheres of cultural influence (government, education, media, marketplace, and so on). These gates become "gates of hell" when Satan takes authority there.

The only way the gates of hell prevail against the church is if one of two things happen: (1) the church abandons the gates, or (2) the church doesn't use the right key to open the gates. It is up to the church to go to the gates of hell (mission) and use the proper kingdom keys (biblical truths) to open the gates wide so our great King can rule. It's time for the church to show back up at the gates and use the keys of the kingdom to open them (Matthew 16:18–19).

None of this happens if there's disunity in the church. But focusing on unity alone is pointless—we must focus on mission. This creates what we call functional unity. Unity is a gift from God when the church properly functions on mission for Him by showing up at the gates of culture. Functional unity is what draws the Marines so close. They don't get together just to fellowship—they get together to fight. The function is the fight, and the result is unity. Unity then becomes the by-product of the function.

We cannot overstate the importance of community within the church. Jesus told us that the two greatest commandments are to love the Lord your God and to love others as yourself (Luke 10:27). This is a vertical love for God and a horizontal love for others. The two greatest *commitments* we can make in life fall right in line with the two greatest *commandments*—to commit personally to God (vertical) and to commit corporately to one another (horizontal). Without both of these commitments we don't have a full picture of the cross. The vertical commitment is the anchor that holds the horizontal commitment in place. There's only one problem: the horizontal commitment is very difficult because we have to trust a perfect God to use an imperfect person to accomplish His perfect will. But if we make these two commitments with our whole hearts and are on mission together as the church, then unity will happen naturally. The gates of hell will not prevail against a unified church willing to follow Jesus to the gates, whatever the cost.

Growing in these two commitments is so important to God that He blesses us with the one thing that will strengthen them both: *trials!* Oh boy, this is the tough part. In 2 Chronicles 32, King Hezekiah was leading Israel in a great reformation, yet God sent an invading army against them. You would think that God would grant them peace and prosperity because their hearts were fully devoted to Him, but the opposite happened. Why? Trials accomplish two things: (1) they draw us closer to God, and (2) they draw us closer to others. Trials reveal our deep need for God's grace and give us an opportunity to witness God's strength working on our behalf through other people. They also reveal to us that we can't make it on our own, and only through the collective whole do we make one perfect body. Trials strengthen our commitment to God and to others in the same way that working out strengthens our muscles—the strain is what strengthens.

Oswald Chambers puts it better than we ever could: "God does not give us overcoming life; He gives us life as we overcome. The strain is the strength. If there is no strain, there is no strength. Are you asking God to give you life and liberty and joy? He cannot, unless you will accept the strain. Immediately you face the strain, you will get the strength."[1] This is all part of the corporate battle within the church.

Third is the *kingdom battle.* This is the fight that will ensue when we seek to advance the comprehensive rule of God in every sphere of life, including government, media, religion, family, entertainment, the marketplace, education, and the arts. The way you know it's a kingdom battle is when you see God being systematically removed and replaced in these areas. Wherever Satan is gaining authority and setting up fortresses, he threatens the church to stay out! The church has, for the most part, neglected the kingdom battlefield over the past several decades, which is why Satan has achieved so much authority at the gates of our culture today. As they used to say at NASA, "Houston, we have a problem."

The bottom line is that Satan wants us stuck in the first two battlefields. If he can defeat us in the personal battle and create disunity in the corporate battle, then we can't fight him in the kingdom battle. We'll be useless in *occupying* until Christ's return.

Here's the key: the more victorious we are in the personal battle and the more united we are in the corporate battle, the more prepared we are to fight the kingdom battle. Yet many of the sermons preached today deal only with the first two battlefields, *personal* and *corporate,* while many of the sermons in the 1700s—the years leading up to American independence—included *kingdom* and dealt with all three equally. This is what it took from God's leaders to help build a nation that has been a safe haven and a launching pad for the gospel for more than 235 years. We pray God's people would face the fear of being mischaracterized by the media, die to their dreams and ideas of success, and live powerfully in the face of increasing opposition today.

THROUGHOUT OUR JOURNEY WE'VE LEARNED SOME OF THE tactics that Satan uses for stealing our power and leaving us useless on these three battlefields. We've seen him use two weapons of choice time and time again. He wants to *scare* us away or *lure* us away from the fight. He wants us to run away from our fears and fully embrace our dreams.

First, he tries to *scare* us away from the fight. He threatens us with fear and intimidation. That is exactly why the Scripture tells us over and over again "do not fear" and "do not be afraid." Satan wants us to live in constant fear, but God wants us to take courage in Him and face our fears—"For God has not given us a spirit of fear and timidity, but of power, love, and self-discipline" (2 Timothy 1:7 NLT). The beauty of having Christ in our hearts is that all we have to do is *face* our fear— and when we face it, God will *fight* it.

If Satan can't scare you into silence, then he'll step up his efforts and try to make you look like a fool. This is what happened to us. We first heard his threats for us to shut up or else. But when that didn't work, he went after our reputations and tried to make us look like fools. That's also a scary thing because no Christian wants the "anti-" label.

Forgive us for using another baseball analogy here, but after going through this situation, we learned that the external blessings we receive from God are just the minor leagues. The big leagues of blessing come when we have the honor of being ridiculed and mistreated for His name's sake (Matthew 5:11–12). Jesus says that when we are persecuted for being a Christian, we are blessed and should rejoice. We should not fear persecution—we should face it and rejoice in it because we know the greatest blessings come on the other side of our greatest fears. When we learn to stand in the face of those fears, we will live powerfully for Jesus. The moment we comprehended this truth was as if God said to us, *Welcome to the big leagues, boys!*

Second, the devil wants to *lure* us away from the fight. If he can't scare us away, then he'll try to lure us away with blessings. We call these our dreams: the purposes, promises, and platforms God gives to us. Our dreams could be a job, our education, a ministry calling, anything we feel *called* to—all of these are good things, but when they become our focus, they become idols. An idol can be anything that impedes or impairs God's rightful place in our lives. And in case you didn't know, God doesn't like idols. The apostle John knew how tempting it would be to replace God when he warned us, "Little children, guard yourselves from idols" (1 John 5:21).

 It's easy to lie to ourselves as to whether or not our dreams have become an idol by saying, "It's all for God's glory." But a dream only has to slightly impede or impair God's rightful position for it to become an idol, even if it doesn't completely overtake His place.

When we focus on the purpose of God instead of on the Person of God, we are easily lured away from following Him whatever the cost. If the things we do—even good things—become idols in our lives, we must die to them. We must not embrace them. Satan knows if he can lure us away by tempting us to hold on to our dreams instead of holding on to God, then he can defeat us. Holding everything with an open hand allows God the freedom to take us wherever He wants to take us.

God may give us dreams and plans for things He wants us to do for His glory. Having a dream motivates us to action. But we can't move the Person of God to the side and replace Him with our newfound purpose or dream. This would be like a ship getting rid of its anchor—when the storm comes, we'll be thrown and tossed.

But when we face our fears and die to our dreams, we will live power- fully. Note that we didn't say, "we *must* live powerfully." We said, "we *will* live powerfully." Living powerfully comes from facing our fears and dying to our dreams. This creates a whatever-the-cost mind-set, and powerful living is the natural result.

WE KNOW WHAT IT'S LIKE TO BE AFRAID. AND WE KNOW WHAT IT'S like to fully embrace a dream. But throughout our lives we've seen the incredible power that Jesus gives when we face our fears and die to our dreams. Whatever the cost to our lives or our reputations—whatever the cost to our dreams and ideas of success—if we stay true to Jesus, then we will live powerfully for Him.

All around you the battle is being waged on three battlegrounds—personal, corporate, and kingdom. And Satan attacks three ways—distracts, deceives, and divides. To try to keep us out of the fight, Satan uses the weapons of ungodly *fear* and ambitious *dreams*—two ditches on either side of the narrow way of Jesus. Each battleground needs men and women who are willing to face their fears, die to their dreams, and live powerfully for Jesus whatever the cost. When we do this, God's authority—His dominion—steps onto the field of battle and defeats Satan every time.

When God put Adam on the earth, He told him to take dominion of the garden, but he couldn't do it without a fight. He lost dominion because of his silence. So the question is, in what garden has God placed you? Where has God given you dominion? And are you fighting God's battles or just keeping quiet as Adam did?

In your personal life, make Jesus your Lord—let Him have total control. In your family, be the leader God has called you to be. In the church, recognize that you weren't meant to fight alone and unite with others to overcome Satan. And in your city and nation, go to the gates and bring God's kingdom there—in the unique way He's created you to do it.

If you're looking for specific ways to prepare yourself for the spiritual battles in life, see Appendix A. In that section are ten action points we've learned that may be helpful to you. In Appendix B all our highlighted principles are in one place, which we hope will help you in your journey.

God has destined us to live powerful lives. Our heavenly Father stands ready to embrace us when we cross the finish line. But until then we must fight, together!

Fight for our faith.
Fight for our families.
Fight for our city.
Fight for our nation.
Fight for our world!

And if we go down, we will go down standing up in the name of Jesus, *whatever the cost!*

ACTION POINTS FOR THE FIGHT

1. READ GOD'S WORD. Spend time in the Bible daily. A good practice is not to let yourself eat until you've first read your Bible—your hunger will drive you to read. And read the Old Testament! There are deep wells of wisdom there. You can join us as we study the Bible; just go to our website, BenhamBrothers.com/Bible, or you can download our BenhamBrothers.com/App. Staying in God's Word will be the best decision of your life.

2. PRAY. There are three steps to prayer: (1) *keep watch*—look and listen for God in all things at all times, (2) *pray without ceasing*—always have a conversation with God, even when you're not alone, and (3) *act*—get up and act on what God speaks to you in prayer. God will do His part, and we must do our part.

3. CHURCH. Join a local community of believers who are *being* the church in your city. You need to be around Christians who are fully engaged in their local communities, not just huddling in a building a few times a week.

4. DISCIPLESHIP. Have an upstream and a downstream. This means committing to being discipled by someone and also discipling others. If you don't have both, then you will miss God's best for you.

5. SHARE. Look for opportunities to share God's love to others everywhere you go. Pray that God makes you a laborer because the harvest is plentiful (Luke 10:2).

6. INPUTS. Consistently measure your inputs. The devil has access to us in two ways: our eyes and our ears. Take daily inventory of what you're watching, reading, and listening to and measure it against the time you spend watching, reading, and listening to God. Don't spend three hours a day watching your favorite shows if you're only spending thirty minutes a day with the Lord.

7. WIND UP. Find out when you wind up and when you wind down, like a clock. Choose to spend time with the Lord when you're wound up because if you do it when you wind down, you'll just fall asleep—every time.

8. GATES. Go to the gates of your city and stand for Jesus. Today, this means going where Satan has taken authority. God has given you a specific key to His kingdom authority, but you have to use it. And you must support other believers who have keys to authority at various gates in our nation as well, such as political leaders, entertainers, educators, business leaders, and so on. Do not be silent at the city gates!

9. BE SALTY. Commit to simply being salty wherever you go (Matthew 5:13–16). Salt and light do not change characteristics based on location and context, so simply be who God made you to be right where He has placed you. This means some people will love the way you taste while others can't stand you.

10. WALK IN REPENTANCE. When you sin, confess it to God and then make it right with others. Walking in repentance means that you earnestly desire to see justice done (2 Corinthians 7:11). This means that once you're vertically right with God, you must get horizontally right with people. The world will take note of this and seek the God we serve. This also includes our duty to stand up for those who cannot stand for themselves. Walking in repentance breathes life into your city.

BENHAM PRINCIPLES

THROUGHOUT THE BOOK WE HIGHLIGHTED SOME LESSONS AND principles we have learned along the way. We thought it might be helpful to see all of those in one place. It helps us too!

1. Your greatest weakness is often an overextension of your greatest strength. To whatever degree you can be strong in one direction, you can be equally weak in the other. The key is to be pointed in the right direction with the right amount of restraint keeping your weaknesses in check.

2. It isn't necessary for kids to learn from the school of hard knocks. Wisdom from parents can save children a lot of heartache. A wise person learns from his mistakes, but one who is even wiser learns from someone else's.

3. As Christians, our work is our worship. The Hebrew word for worship—*avodah*—is also the same word used for work. Our work becomes worship when we do it with all of our might for the glory of the Lord.

4. We cannot give what we do not possess. It's impossible to pass on to our children something we don't truly possess ourselves. This is what it takes to create an appetite in our children for the things of God. The things that are caught are far more powerful than the things that are taught.

5. You will accomplish a lot more in the pain cave than the comfort zone. The only way to maintain a disciplined lifestyle is to get comfortable with discomfort. It's like the difference between an adrenaline rush and an endorphin release. Adrenaline is the fight-or-flight feeling that happens quickly and wears off fast. An endorphin release, on the other hand, happens slowly and lasts for a long time—yet it only occurs through pain. Runners call this the "runner's high." Life is best lived off the endorphins of peace through pain and not off the adrenaline from one rush to the next.

6. There are two ways to win: on the scoreboard and off the scoreboard. We all want to win *on* the scoreboard, but true winners win *off* the scoreboard too—which means to win over yourself. This is the most important victory. If you win on the scoreboard and lose over yourself, you've lost that day. But if you lose on the scoreboard and win over yourself, you've won that day. It's important to try to win both ways, but winning over yourself is by far the more important victory.

7. True surrender means Jesus is Savior *and* Lord. It's one thing to confess Jesus as Savior but another thing to confess Him as Lord. If He is Lord, then He is ruler of all—including our time, talents, and treasure. Jesus doesn't just want to save us and stack us up at a spiritual bus stop, waiting for Him to pick us up. He wants us to occupy until He returns. He wants us to live powerfully for Him with whatever He's given us to do, in the unique way He's equipped us to do it.

8. James 4:7 says, "Resist the devil, and he will flee from you." You cannot properly resist Satan unless you're willing through the power of Christ to face him first. This starts in your own life personally and then moves to your home, community, and nation. Though his fists will be flying at your face, you must never turn your back on Satan. When you face him with resistance, you have the power of God to defeat him.

9. Dreams don't accomplish themselves. It requires discipline to make your dream a reality. When a baseball player hits a 95 mph fastball, he's able to do this through endless hours of disciplined practice. Everyone dreams, but not everyone accomplishes. The difference is in personal discipline.

10. As we focus on depth, God will handle breadth. Our one role is to go deep with God and be faithful right where He has planted us. We don't need to worry about how wide or high our branches are going to grow—we just need to focus on how deep our roots go. He'll handle the breadth of our branches as we focus on depth in Him.

11. God always pays for what He orders. As He orders your steps, He will work behind the scenes for you to make the way. And He does it in ways and with people you would never imagine. All you have to do is trust Him and be at rest.

12. Your talent can be either a tool or a toy. Glorifying God with your talent makes it a useful tool. Glorifying yourself with your talent makes it a useless toy. Tools help others. Toys help only you. God wants our talents to be His tools, not our toys.

13. The goal of sports is first to develop character and second to develop talent. The more coaches and parents understand this, the more

competition will build others up and not tear others down. The same holds true for education—the goal is first to develop character and then to deliver content.

14. The goal of prayer is not to simply get an answer from God—it's to get to know the God of the answer. Drawing near to God in prayer develops a relational connection that forges our union with Him in stone. And when He answers in a big way—it's just icing on the cake!

15. Christians in the marketplace—or anywhere for that matter—should be characterized by excellence. When a hair stylist shares the gospel while cutting hair, which part is ministry: sharing the gospel or cutting the hair? We say *both!* Excellence in business provides a solid platform for incredible ministry.

16. Being results-focused tends to cause us to think strategically in our minds as opposed to spiritually in our hearts. However, when we focus on our duty (from the heart) and not the results (in our minds), we can operate both strategically and spiritually in our duty while God handles all the results.

17. When we focus on being faithful to what God has given us to do in the present, we can trust He will orchestrate what He wants for us in the future. We don't have to worry about the future—we just have to be faithful in the present.

18. We often spend life chasing success but not stopping to define it. Yet what we call the journey God calls success. As a Christian, success is not a destination—it's the journey. When you go through the trials of life and remain true to God, you are a living example of success, regardless of your destination.

19. When God gives you something, you must hold it with an open hand. Otherwise, if He decides to remove it, He'll have to pry your fingers loose. Holding your dreams with an open hand requires that you focus on the God of the dream and *not* the dream that God gives.

20. Dying to our dreams is only possible when we focus on the *Person* of God and not the *purposes, promises,* or *platforms* He gives us. By focusing on the Person, we sit loose to how, when, and where His purposes, promises, or platforms are given or taken from us. This gives us the ability to live powerfully for God, especially through trials.

21. Proverbs 16:7 says, "When a man's ways are pleasing to the LORD, / He makes even his enemies to be at peace with him." Although our *words* will not always please people when speaking God's truth, our *ways* should be pleasing to them. The way we live (or play baseball) should help, not hinder, the words of our mouths.

22. The same boiling water that hardens the egg softens the carrot. It's not the water that makes the difference—it's the substance of what's in the water. As a Christian, your life will harden some people and soften others. You don't have to worry which one it is—you just stay hot for Christ and let Him take care of the rest.

23. It's really important to check your motives any time you want to do something for God. You will know your motive by how you respond when someone notices what you're doing—do you swell with pride or are you graced with humility? When the motive is pure, it's always graced with humility.

24. One of the biggest dangers for men is to find their identities in what they *do* as opposed to who they *are*. When what you do defines you,

then your career longings will naturally pull you away from God and from those He's given to your care. But as Christians we can rest in the fact that we are not defined by the jobs we hold in our hands—we are defined by the One who holds us in His hand.

25. We are human *beings*, not human *doings*. In Christ, we are a new creation, so *being* faithful no matter what we *do* for a living gives us the ability to live powerfully for Jesus because our identities are found in Him alone.

26. When God places something in your hand, don't grab ahold of it. Let Him keep it there if He sees fit. Just like the earth has a gravitational pull that keeps things in place, so God will keep things in our hands that He wants there. We don't have to wrap our fingers around it.

27. Our sweet spot in life is where our greatest talent and our greatest passion intersect. While this is true, we need to be careful not to see the sweet spot for our lives as simply a destination. It's also a state of being. We like to say, make your spot sweet wherever you are. No matter where your season of life finds you, you can make your spot sweet when you fix your eyes on Jesus.

28. Psalm 37:4 doesn't mean we get a red Porsche if our hearts desire it. It means that if we delight in the Lord—love what He loves—then our desires begin to reflect His desires. And when this happens, we can simply follow the desires of our hearts because our desires will be properly aligned with His desires.

29. Faithfulness is proved in the ordinary. We've heard it said that God uses ordinary people to do extraordinary things, and that's true. But God also uses extraordinary people to do very ordinary things. Faithfulness to God is tested in the fires of the ordinary.

30. Working from the heart unlocks God's supernatural favor on our work. Every little thing we do—plunging toilets, washing cars, homeschooling kids, chairing the board, or hitting home runs—if done for the Lord from our hearts, will be rewarded. God will take the natural and make it supernatural only if we're willing to give our very best for Him.

31. When God wants to move you from one place to another, He does it through a *push* and a *pull*. There will be both a push from where you are *and* a pull to where you need to be. Often we make our decisions when we feel either a push *or* a pull, but rarely do we wait for both.

32. There are two aspects to waiting on God: the *state* of waiting and the *service* of waiting. The state of waiting involves looking and listening for God in all things and at all times—actively waiting for His lead. The service of waiting is the opportunity to serve while we wait. It's very important to engage in the service of waiting while we remain faithful in the state of waiting.

33. On two occasions when the disciples told Jesus there was a need for food, He turned and asked what *they* had to provide. In the same way, when we see needs and have needs, our first response should be to see what's in our own bags. God wants us to use the talents and tools He's put in our bags, whatever they may be. The more faithful we are with those, the more God can supernaturally bless them to meet our needs and the needs of others.

34. Providing for your family's immediate needs while simultaneously moving toward your goals forces you to work hard and trust God— two vital components of every good man.

35. Going the second mile is one of the most powerful tools in business. Going the first mile fulfills your obligation, but going the

second mile opens the door to share your faith. If you meet the physical need you're getting paid for, then you will have an open door to meet the spiritual need you're not getting paid for. The path to meeting spiritual needs in the marketplace is first to meet their physical needs in a supernatural way.

36. There's a direct connection between personal purity and professional performance. Step one of any business should be to evaluate motives and analyze improper actions or attitudes before God. Before looking at systems and process, it's best to start looking into our hearts because impurity blocks the favor of God. External favor rests in internal purity.

37. Work is a beautiful thing—it existed before Adam sinned. When we complete the work God has given us to do, we can experience the rest God has ordained for us. The *requirement* for work is faithfulness. The *reward* for work is rest. The *result* of work is that God is glorified.

38. The principle of delayed gratification means you're willing to forgo the temporary enjoyment of something today for the permanent enjoyment of something tomorrow. The money earned in the early years of a business is "seed" money, which should always go back into the ground. Too often business owners see their initial earnings as "harvest"—and they reap it prematurely. This is why so many businesses fail in the first five years.

39. First *who* then *what*. We hire according to *who* and not *what*. What people know about a job is not nearly as important as who they are. As our business grew, we looked to hire the right *who*, knowing we could easily teach them *what* to do.

40. One of the first commands God gave Adam was to work. Work existed before sin existed. The way Adam worshiped God was to be

faithful in the work God called him to do. Whether it was pruning trees, trimming shrubs, or naming animals, Adam's one responsibility was to be faithful in the work God had given him to do. God was responsible for *what* Adam's work was—Adam was responsible for *how* he did it.

41. When ambition takes the lead, the ends justify the means so that accomplishing the thing is more important than the way we accomplish it. Ambition is meant to follow and strengthen, not lead and dominate.

42. Faithfulness in your career sets a proper foundation for effectiveness in your calling. Often your career paves the way for your calling. Be faithful here, and you'll be effective there.

43. God's *yes* doesn't always mean God's *go*. *Yes* is permission—*go* is a command. Wisdom waits for both a *yes* and a *go* from God before moving forward.

44. How we see ourselves determines how we conduct ourselves. This is why Satan attacks Christians at the level of their identities. He knows that if we see ourselves as ministers, then we will act like ministers. He's okay with us finding our identities in our vocations, but he doesn't want us to find our identities in who we are in Christ. Once we see ourselves as ministers of God, Satan has no power to stand against us.

45. Bob Fraser in *Marketplace Christianity* said, "If money were *water*, then riches would be a *bucket* of water, and wealth a *river* of water."[1] Gathering riches to be given is one thing, but generating wealth to be given is another. Wealth is sustainable while riches are not.

46. Owners have two rights: the right to possess and the right to do whatever they want with what they possess (within the law, of course). They can keep what they own or give it away—it doesn't matter because they own it. Stewards, on the other hand, have possession but no ownership rights associated with it. Even though they maintain possession, they must do with it what the owner desires, period.

47. Truth is a Person, and love is the same Person, whose name is Jesus. To be either one or the other is to divide Christ. Love without truth is not biblical love, and truth without love is not biblical truth. More importantly, one without the other is not Jesus. We *can* and *should be* both.

48. Concerning ourselves with perception (what people say about us) makes man-pleasers. Concerning ourselves with reality (what God says about us) makes God-pleasers. We must not concern ourselves with the lies or the applause of man but only with what God says is true. Perception is not reality—reality is reality.

49. Authority follows responsibility. The way to receive authority is to stand in your proper place of responsibility. If you abandon your responsibility, you forfeit your authority. Consider fatherlessness in America—when men forsake their responsibility in the home, they lose authority in culture. Evil gains authority in a nation when men refuse to stand in their place of responsibility in the home.

50. It's one thing to be against murder (abortion), but it's another thing to bring life. That's what Jesus does—He defeats death and He brings life. One of the core business principles we teach is to breathe life. We say "breathe" life because it should come as naturally to us as breathing—that wherever we go, we "breathe"

the life of Jesus into our city. This is what being profitable truly looks like.

51. How you see the battle determines how you fight it. If you see it as a physical battle only, then you will pick up the wrong weapon, just as Peter did when he cut off the ear of the servant to the high priest (John 18:10). But if you see it as a spiritual one, then you will pick up the right weapon and fight it with the right weapon—truth and love. You can't be in the Spirit and be hateful at the same time.

52. It's natural to let the *purpose* of God replace the *Person* of God. This only happens when our focus is on the purpose of God and not the God of purpose. When we do this, we begin transacting with God at the level of the mind and no longer at the level of the heart. Things then have to make sense for us before we follow God, and strategy overtakes the Spirit. But when our focus remains on the Person of God and we let His purposes follow in the wake, then we will transact with Him at the level of the heart. We'll obey Him whatever the cost even if it doesn't make sense in our minds. We seek to live Person-driven lives—we let the Person of God take control of His purposes for us.

53. Twelve things we learned during this time:
    (1) When a vision is birthed and we die to it, if it resurrects itself, we need to stay dead to it in our hearts.
    (2) Don't let a thirst for influence turn into a lust for influence. We need to go after the God of influence and not the influence that God gives.
    (3) Ambition is a great follower but a terrible leader. We need to die to selfish ambition.
    (4) We need to keep focusing on depth and let God handle our breadth.

(5) We need to be faithful to keep doing what we've always done and not move on to the next thing (pick the broomstick back up and be faithful in little things).

(6) When *want* enters the picture—we want things we didn't used to want—remember this: "The Lord is my shepherd, / I shall *not* want" (Psalm 23:1).

(7) Being wanted feels good, but it can lead to being a people-pleaser.

(8) Being a "living" sacrifice (Romans 12:1) is all about faithfulness because when the heat turns up, we want to hop off the altar.

(9) Reframe! We need to reframe difficult situations in our minds— is it really so bad? Not in light of all the pain Christ went through for us.

(10) Be careful not to fear man more than God—being worried about what people think instead of what God thinks.

(11) We must decrease, and He must increase. Avoid the temptation to think we must increase so He can increase. That's dumb!

(12) Emotions take time—healing often happens long before you *feel* healed.

54. Boldness apart from brokenness makes a bully. God must first break us so that He can use us. He did the same with Peter, and on the foundation of Peter's brokenness God used him to help build the church, even though he denied Him three times. A broken man is a powerful man, one who can be as bold as a lion.

55. Iron sharpens iron (Proverbs 27:17); marshmallows don't sharpen marshmallows. For iron to be sharpened it must clash with another piece of iron—this is healthy. Spiritual and intellectual progress stops the minute you silence one side of the debate. We all need to toughen up a bit and let our ideas clash for the health of the church and the nation.

56. The secret to experiencing the power of God in your life is through total surrender. This means giving everything we have to God, whatever the cost. Sometimes our decision to surrender to Jesus may cost others, too, which is precisely why many of us hold back. We may not mind paying the price of total surrender ourselves, but it's very difficult when others have to pay it as well.

57. Christians in the marketplace are to operate according to a covenant and not simply a contract. Contracts are based on mutual shielding (ensuring that you *get* what you deserve), but covenants are based on mutual yielding (ensuring that you *give* what you have).

58. There are many cultural pressures to live according to the world's way today, but focusing on what God thinks and not what others think allows you to live from the inside out instead of the outside in. This eternal perspective allows you to live powerfully, even in the face of fears.

59. We all love it when God uses people's strengths to get us where He wants us, but it's much more difficult when He uses their weaknesses to do it. With an eternal perspective we clearly see that God can and will use *anything* and *anyone* to accomplish His purposes in our lives. We shouldn't get upset if He uses someone's weakness to do the job. If we focus on God's strength as opposed to their weakness, then we'll receive the blessing without the burden of resentment.

60. God is not going to give you what's in His hand until you let go of what's in yours. The issue isn't, what's in God's hand? The issue is, do you trust God enough to let go of what's in yours?

61. Freedom is not the ability to *get* what you *want*, but it's the ability to *give* what you *have*. When you do that, you are truly free.

62. It's easy to lie to ourselves as to whether or not our dreams have become an idol by saying, "It's all for God's glory." But a dream only has to slightly impede or impair God's rightful position for it to become an idol, even if it doesn't completely overtake His place.

CITIES4LIFE™ CODE OF CONDUCT

PRAY

OUR PURPOSE IS TO GLORIFY OUR LORD AND SAVIOR, JESUS CHRIST. We are here to bring our prayers and supplications to our heavenly Father in the name of Jesus Christ. We are here to minister in a prayerful presence that it is unlawful to destroy the life of the unborn child. We are here to represent the love and mercy that God extends to sinners, and we pray for mercy on the unborn children scheduled to die. We are here to support those who are proclaiming the gospel and speaking the Truth in love to mothers, their friends and families, and clinic personnel and will pray specifically for any immediate needs we see in front of the abortion centers. We must remember to be prompted by the Holy Spirit to pray as He leads us. Our duty is to faithfully lay our requests before His throne, trusting that His will be done.

PROCLAIM

OUR PURPOSE IS TO GLORIFY OUR LORD AND SAVIOR, JESUS CHRIST. We are here to proclaim the truth of the gospel. We are here as witnesses to the biblical truth that it is unlawful to destroy the life of an unborn child. We are here to expose the lies and evil deeds of the abortion industry. We are here to proclaim that abortion is an act of violence that kills an unborn child in the womb of his/her mother. We are here to offer help and hope and truth to people entering and exiting the abortion clinic. Participants *must* be peaceful, prayerful, and nonviolent. Participants must be willing to follow instructions of leadership within Cities4Life. Only one designated counselor at a time should speak out to people entering and exiting the killing center. Participants must not be argumentative with patients, clinic personnel, police officers, or others. We must remember that the Holy Spirit is the One who convicts each person of sin. Our duty is to faithfully witness and proclaim the truth, leaving the results in the hands of our Sovereign Lord.

PROVIDE

OUR PURPOSE IS TO GLORIFY OUR LORD AND SAVIOR, JESUS CHRIST. We exist to provide tangible support to women and families in need as Scripture commands. All services and ministry provided to these mothers is to be done in a Christlike way, allowing the gifts of time, services, or goods to make way for the Giver. We believe in the unity within the body of Christ as we serve alongside one another to fulfill the Great Commission and Jesus' promise of being known among the lost by our love one for another.

I AGREE TO THESE PEACEFUL TERMS OF SERVICE:

Print Name: _____

Signature: _____

Date: _____

This is a Christian ministry centered upon the gospel of Jesus Christ:
http://cities4life.org/assets/code-of-conduct-1.pdf

ACKNOWLEDGMENTS

PRESSURE PRECEDES PERSECUTION. WHEN ONE GENERATION refuses to stand up to the pressure, the next generation will reap the persecution. In America today we are simply experiencing religious pressure, and if we don't stand strong, religious persecution is right around the corner. Yet despite it all, the kingdom of God still advances. We want to acknowledge all those who have suffered intense persecution for their faith and yet stood strong, whatever the cost.

And to our writer, Scott Lamb, you made this project possible. Making sense out of one thousand pages of material and channeling the energy of two hardheaded twins is not a job for the faint of heart. Big hug, leg wrap, scream-cry—from the bottom of our hearts.

NOTES

CHAPTER 3: YOUNG WARRIOR SPIRITS

1. William D. Bjoraker, "Word Study: (AVODAH)—Work/Worship," Assemblies of God: Evangelism, Worship, Discipleship, and Compassion, http://ag.org/top/church_workers/wrshp_gen_avodah.cfm.

CHAPTER 4: CREATE THE CRAVE

1. Adrian Rogers, "Raising Young Champions," Love Worth Finding with Adrian Rogers, oneplace.com, http://www.oneplace.com/ministries/love-worth-finding/read/articles/raising-young-champions-11094.html.

CHAPTER 6: LIBERTY U

1. John Nogowski, "Matters of Faith Sometimes Not That Far Afield," *Tallahassee Democrat*, May 26, 1998.

CHAPTER 8: FROM A BASEBALL BAT TO A BROOMSTICK

1. A. W. Tozer, *The Root of the Righteous* (Camp Hill, PA: Christian Publications, 1986), 137.

CHAPTER 9: FINDING FORECLOSURE

1. Phil Robertson tells a similar story about "fishing the river" in his book with Mark Schlabach, *Happy, Happy, Happy: My Life and Legacy as the Duck Commander* (Nashville: Howard, 2013), 122.
2. Dave Ramsey, *The Total Money Makeover: A Proven Plan for Financial Fitness* (Nashville: Thomas Nelson, 2009), 5.

3. *Merriam-Webster Collegiate Dictionary*, 11th ed. (Springfield, MA: Merriam-Webster, 2003), s.v. "pure."

CHAPTER 11: IF THE FOUNDATIONS ARE DESTROYED

1. Ravi Zacharias, "If the Foundations Be Destroyed: Part 1 of 4," *Just Thinking* (podcast), September 2, 2013, 11:00–12:30, http://www.rzim .org/just-thinking-broadcasts/if-the-foundations-be-destroyed-part -1-of-4/.
2. Ibid.

CHAPTER 12: MISSIONEERING

1. Tony Evans, *America: Turning a Nation to God* (Chicago: Moody, 2015).
2. Robert Fraser, *Marketplace Christianity: Discovering the Kingdom Purpose of the Marketplace* (Grandview, MO: Oasis House, 2004), 68; emphasis in original.

CHAPTER 13: PRAYING FOR RESTORATION

1. Martin Luther King Jr., *Strength to Love* (Minneapolis, MN: Fortress Press, 2010), 59.
2. John Adams, "Proclamation 8—Recommending a National Day of Humiliation, Fasting, and Prayer," March 23, 1798, online by Gerhard Peters and John T. Wooley, *The American Presidency Project*, http://www .presidency.ucsb.edu/ws/?pid=65661.
3. William Martin, A. Larry Ross, and Michael Hamilton, "Has Billy Graham Suddenly Turned Political?" *Christianity Today*, October 19, 2012, http://www.christianitytoday.com/ct/2012/october-web-only/billy -graham-political-statements-history.html.
4. "Charlotte714 Recap Film," Benham Companies, http://www .benhamcompanies.com/initiative/charlotte714.
5. Billy Graham, "Why Don't Churches Practice Brotherhood?" *Reader's Digest*, August 1960, 55.
6. "Charlotte714 Recap Film," Benham Companies.

CHAPTER 14: BREATHE LIFE INTO YOUR CITY

1. Martin Luther King Jr., *Strength to Love* (Minneapolis, MN: Fortress Press, 2010), 59.
2. David Benham, *Janet Mefferd Show*, "Hour 3—David Benham Talks about Charlotte714," http://www.janetmefferdpremium .com/2012/09/05/janet-mefferd-radio-show-20120905-hr-3/.

3. Brian Tashman, "Charlotte Prayer Rally Repents for 'Homosexuality and its Agenda that is Attacking the Nation,'" Right Wing Watch, September 6, 2012, http://www.rightwingwatch.org/content/charlotte-prayer-rally-homosexuality-agenda-nation.
4. North Carolina State Center for Health Statistics, "Reported Pregnancies 2012," http://www.schs.state.nc.us/schs/data/pregnancies/2012.
5. Cities4Life, "Code of Conduct," http://cities4life.org/assets/code-of-conduct-1.pdf.

CHAPTER 17: DYING AGAIN

1. Brian Tashman, "HGTV Picks Anti-Gay, Anti-Choice Extremist for New Reality TV Show," Right Wing Watch, May 6, 2014, http://www.rightwingwatch.org/content/hgtv-picks-anti-gay-anti-choice-extremists-new-reality-tv-show.
2. David Benham and Jason Benham, "Statement on HGTV," BenhamBrothers.com, May 8, 2014, http://benhambrothers.com/statement.

CHAPTER 18: RUNNING THROUGH FIRST BASE

1. David Benham and Jason Benham, "Finishing What We Started," BenhamBrothers.com, July 9, 2014, http://benhambrothers.com/finishing-started.
2. J. R. R. Tolkien, Lord of the Rings: The Two Towers (Crows Nest, New South Wales: George Allen and Unwin, 1954), chapter 6.
3. ABC News, Nightline, May 10, 2014, 12:37–1:08 a.m. PDT, https://archive.org/details/KGO_20140510_073700_Nightline.

CHAPTER 19: BATTLE READY

1. Oswald Chambers, My Utmost for His Highest, "The Discipline of Difficulty," August 2, http://utmost.org/classic/the-discipline-of-difficulty-classic/.

APPENDIX B

1. Robert Fraser, Marketplace Christianity: Discovering the Kingdom Purpose of the Marketplace (Grandview, MO: Oasis House, 2004), 68; emphasis in original.

ABOUT THE AUTHORS

DAVID AND JASON BENHAM, FORMER PROFESSIONAL BASEBALL players, are also nationally acclaimed entrepreneurs. The twin brothers' business success earned them a reality show with HGTV, set to air during the 2014 fall season. Due to their commitment to traditional and biblical values, however, the show was abruptly canceled. The Benhams immediately found themselves in the midst of a cultural firestorm, but they refused to back down and decided to stand and fight for what they believe.

The brothers' first company was recognized as one of *Inc.* magazine's Fastest Growing Private Companies, and they've been awarded Ernst & Young's Entrepreneur of the Year Finalists, *Wall Street Journal's* Top Real Estate Professionals, and Business Leader Media's Top 50 Entrepreneurs. They were also named Franchise 500's Top New Franchise.

Appearing on CNN, Fox News, TheBlaze, ABC's *Nightline, Good Morning America,* and others, the Benhams continue to stand up for what they believe. After their show was canceled the Benhams trended nationally on social media, and more than 51 million tweets about the Benham brands have been delivered to Twitter streams.

David and Jason are happily married, and their families live on the same street in Charlotte, North Carolina. Their wives, Lori and Tori, homeschool their combined nine children and are passionate about serving in their community.

Follow David and Jason on Twitter:
@DavidDBenham
@JasonBBenham
Visit their website: BenhamBrothers.com